U.S. MARINES AT THE BATTLE FOR SANGIN

"Incredible on all levels. This book encompasses the powerful resilience of Marines through the most extreme experiences and reading it challenged me to be a better person. Inspiring from cover to cover and well worth the read."
– CLAY RUDICK, Founder & CEO

"A gripping memoir that is both intellectually and emotionally engaging. Landon writes with authenticity, honesty, and a level of quality that effectively captures his wartime experiences. I walked away with a greater understanding and appreciation for Marines and found myself deeply moved by many of the events described in the book."
– ZACK HEMSEY, Recording Artist

"One of the purest tellings of a combat Marine's experience in warfighting I have ever read. This story strikes every emotion."
– PAUL LONGGREAR, Colonel ret. Army Special Forces, Ranger Hall of Fame Inductee

"Profoundly moving account of the Battle for Sangin that impacted me deeply. I have always held a great respect for Marines, but this book gave me a whole new appreciation for what our young military men and women endure in service to our country."
– DEVIN BARNWELL, Managing Partner, Global Portfolio Manager

U.S. MARINES AT THE BATTLE FOR SANGIN

OPERATION ENDURING FREEDOM

LANDON LONGGREAR

Pen & Sword
MILITARY

AN IMPRINT OF PEN & SWORD BOOKS LTD.
YORKSHIRE – PHILADELPHIA

First published in Great Britain in 2025 by
PEN AND SWORD MILITARY
An imprint of
Pen & Sword Books Limited
Yorkshire – Philadelphia

Copyright © Landon Longgrear, 2025

ISBN 978 1 03611 677 4

The right of Landon Longgrear to be identified as Author of this work has been asserted by him in accordance with the Copyright, Designs and Patents Act 1988.

A CIP catalogue record for this book is available from the British Library.

All rights reserved. No part of this book may be reproduced, transmitted, downloaded, decompiled or reverse engineered in any form or by any means, electronic or mechanical including photocopying, recording or by any information storage and retrieval system, without permission from the Publisher in writing. NO AI TRAINING: Without in any way limiting the Author's and Publisher's exclusive rights under copyright, any use of this publication to "train" generative artificial intelligence (AI) technologies to generate text is expressly prohibited. The Author and Publisher reserve all rights to license uses of this work for generative AI training and development of machine learning language models.

Typeset in Times New Roman 12/16 by
SJmagic DESIGN SERVICES, India.
Printed and bound in the UK by CPI Group (UK) Ltd.

The Publisher's authorised representative in the EU for product safety is Authorised Rep Compliance Ltd., Ground Floor, 71 Lower Baggot Street, Dublin D02 P593, Ireland.
www.arccompliance.com

For a complete list of Pen & Sword titles please contact
PEN & SWORD BOOKS LIMITED
George House, Units 12 & 13, Beevor Street, Off Pontefract Road,
Barnsley, South Yorkshire, S71 1HN, England
E-mail: enquiries@pen-and-sword.co.uk
Website: www.pen-and-sword.co.uk

or

PEN AND SWORD BOOKS
1950 Lawrence Rd, Havertown, PA 19083, USA
E-mail: uspen-and-sword@casematepublishers.com
Website: www.penandswordbooks.com

For the fallen and their families. For God, Country, and Corps. Most of all for liberty and the privilege to live free of man's tyranny.

'War is among the greatest horrors known to humanity; it should never be romanticized. The means of war is force, applied in the form of organized violence. It is through the use of violence, or the credible threat of violence, that we compel our enemy to do our will. Violence is an essential element of war, and its immediate result is bloodshed, destruction, and suffering. While the magnitude of violence may vary with the object and means of war, the violent essence of war will never change.'[1]

Warfighting,
United States Marine Corps

---

1. United States Government, *Warfighting*, 1997, p.14.

CONTENTS

Author's Note viii
Unit Structure / Rank Structure ix
Glossary of Frequent Terms x
Introduction xii

Chapter 1   In the Beginning 1
Chapter 2   Into the Cauldron 11
Chapter 3   The Big Show 34
Chapter 4   We're Operational 52
Chapter 5   Murder Holes and Killing Fields 72
Chapter 6   Tanks of Sangin 93
Chapter 7   The Tipping Point 112
Chapter 8   Changing Tides 135
Chapter 9   Control the Chaos 150
Chapter 10 War and Humanity 167

For the Fallen 173
Rifleman's Creed 174

AUTHOR'S NOTE

This book is an account of my experiences as a United States Marine involved in the war in Afghanistan, otherwise known as Operation Enduring Freedom. I spent nearly five years and countless hours recalling, corroborating, organizing and reflecting on the details of those experiences to chronicle this war story.

I am convinced that any war story is worth telling provided it allows readers to better understand the gravity of war and the impacts on those who participate in it. Emotional highs and lows, triumphs and defeats, exhilarations and deep struggles across the bandwidth of anyone's wartime experiences make up just small pieces of a big picture that we should all learn from.

I hope this story is a blessing to all who read it, a first hand view of the rigors of war to all who will hopefully never have to experience it, a wholehearted salute to every veteran that has been through it themselves, and a reminder to all people that in this world there are things worth fighting and dying for, and none more so than the establishment, preservation and spread of peaceful life, liberty and the pursuit of happiness for all.

UNIT STRUCTURE

1st Battalion, 23rd Marines – 830 Marines

Alpha Company – 165 Marines

2nd Platoon – 40 Marines

1st Squad – 13 Marines
2nd Squad – 13 Marines
3rd Squad – 13 Marines

RANK STRUCTURE

ENLISTED
E1 – Private (Pvt)
E2 – Private First Class (PFC)
E3 – Lance Corporal (LCpl)
E4 – Corporal (Cpl)
E5 – Sergeant (Sgt)
E6 – Staff Sergeant (SSgt)
E7 – Gunnery Sergeant (GySgt)
E8 – First Sergeant (1stSgt) / Master Sergeant (MSgt)
E9 – Sergeant Major (SgtMaj) / Master Gunnery Sergeant (MGySgt)

OFFICER
O1 – Second Lieutenant
O2 – First Lieutenant
O3 – Captain
O4 – Major
O5 – Lieutenant Colonel
O6 – Colonel
O7 – Brigadier General
O8 – Major General ('2 Star')
O9 – Lieutenant General ('3 Star')
O10 – General ('4 Star')

GLOSSARY OF FREQUENT TERMS

ACOG	Advanced Combat Optical Gunsight (rifle scope).
ACOG Chevron	Chevron is the scope's "crosshairs," which is shaped like a chevron.
AHP	Afghan Highway Patrol.
ANA	Afghan National Army.
ANP	Afghan National Police.
AO	Area of Operation.
AT-4	Anti-Tank shoulder fired rocket.
Battalion (unit)	~830 Marines typically separated into 5 Companies.
C4	Composition 4. Commonly used military explosive material.
Casevac	Casualty Evacuation. Typically refers to evacuating wounded off battlefield.
Click	1 click = 1,000 meters.
COC	Command Operations Center.
COIN Mission	Counter Insurgency.
Company (unit)	~165 Marines separated into 4 Platoons.
CP	Command Post.
Double/Triple Amputee	Permanent loss of 2 or 3 extremities (arms and legs).
DShK	'Degtyarov Shpagin Krupnokalibernyi' (enemy heavy machine gun equivalent to our US Military 50 caliber machine gun).
ECP	Entry Choke Point.
EOD	Explosive Ordinance Disposal (explosives experts).
FOB	Forward Operating Base.
GBU	Guided Bomb Unit (precision guided air-to-ground bomb.
GWOT	Global War on Terror.
ICOM Chatter	Inter Communication (Taliban's internal radio communications).
IED	Improvised Explosive Device.
IDF	Indirect fire (artillery mortars).
IR	Infrared.

GLOSSARY OF FREQUENT TERMS

ISR Drone	Intelligence, Surveillance and Reconnaissance unmanned drone.
KIA	Killed in Action.
LAW Rocket	Light Anti-armor Weapon (shoulder fired rocket).
M240G	US Military "heavy" machine gun. Belt-fed 7.62x51mm bullets.
MAM	Military Aged Male.
MATV	MRAP All Terrain Vehicle.
Medevac	Medical Evacuation. Typically refers to evacuating wounded out of combat zone to medical facility.
MRAP	Mine Resistant Ambush Protected armored truck.
Murder holes	Intentionally carved out holes in thick mud compound walls just large enough to fire weapons through.
Nine Line (9 line)	Standardized casevac request radio report format used to communicate critical information.
NVGs	Night Vision Goggles.
OEF	Operation Enduring Freedom, i.e. the war in Afghanistan.
OP/LP	Observation Post / Listening Post, much smaller than a PB.
PB	Patrol Base, much smaller than a FOB.
PKM	'Pulemyot Kalashnikova Modernizirovannyi' (enemy heavy machine gun equivalent to our US Military M240G machine gun).
Platoon (unit)	~40 Marines separated into 3 Squads.
QRF	Quick Reaction Force.
RIP	Relief in Place.
ROE	Rules of Engagement.
RPG	Rocket Propelled Grenade.
RTB	Return to Base.
SAW	M249 Squad Automatic Weapon. Belt-fed 5.56x45mm bullets.
SMAW	Shoulder-launched Multipurpose Assault Weapon (shoulder fired rocket).
Squad (unit)	~13 Marines separated into 3 Fire teams.
SOPs	Standard Operating Procedures.
Unit	Common general reference to specific group of Marines or combatants of any size.
TIC	Troops in Contact, a radio declaration used to alert command that a unit on the ground is actively engaged in a firefight.
V-BIED	Vehicle Born Improvised Explosive Device.
WIA	Wounded in Action.

INTRODUCTION

The days were longer than I had ever experienced and the pressure at times was insurmountable. High-stakes environments bring the best and worst out of people and this brought both out of me. Nothing mattered more than what was right in front of me. Self-concern diminished as the days went by and mental callousness grew in place. I became increasingly emotionally numb, which was welcomed as it yielded more consistent logical thinking, but that also became strained. Eventually all the repetition turned into thoughtless reaction and the days began cycling through like a machine. I was a Marine at war, bent on decimating the enemy that stood against me. Days were filled with the constant threat of violence and nights were the same. It was an alternate reality in many ways where the priorities that govern daily life were completely different than what I had known in peacetime back home. Mission first, then gear, then other personnel, and then self was the pecking order of importance, and I was not to think twice about it. It was an alignment of priorities that I was trained to live and die by as a foot soldier fighting my nation's war and it came with the broader package I signed up for when I chose to join what I knew to be the fiercest warfighting force in the world.

United States Marines are brought up to be highly refined and aggressively violent. The fighting spirit of Marines in combat has often been characterized by relentless brutality in the path of mission accomplishment. Conventionally, we were not intended to be a small, tactical, precision-hitting force so much as a fraternity of committed battlefield brawlers, eager to get in the fight and slug it out to the last man standing. Courage and resolute commitment to mission accomplishment above all else is the standard and death is to come before compromising that standard. This brute mentality was instilled in me and others from the beginning of my time in the Corps as a continuation of the reputation Marines had established throughout many battles of Marine Corps history. From Bella Wood, the Battle for Okinawa, the Frozen Chosin Reservoir, and Hue City to the door-to-door blood fest of Fallujah, Marines have consistently earned their reputation by having a 'fix bayonets and charge' mind set. I think this is what sets the Corps apart. It is the fundamentally harsh and aggressive nature co-mingled with extreme determination to win that undergirds everything we do. It is also the esprit de corps comradery that orbits the severity of our existence, and the continuation of the warrior culture that past generations established and carried forward to us.

In the Global War on Terror (GWOT) that followed the 9/11/2001 attack on American soil, Marines were at the tip of the spear. We were the far-extended arm of America's defense and were thrown into the firestorm of armed conflict on behalf of our nation. When my time came to deploy, I was as voracious to engage in combat as any Marine before me. It was the pinnacle of my very limited youthful aspirations and the culmination of my preceding years of violence in Marine Corps training. I was young and naive but had a good head on my shoulders and a heart that wanted to do good in this world. Both were put to the test in the fray of the war in Afghanistan.

In early 2011, I landed in what eventually earned the reputation of being the bloodiest battle campaign of the entire twenty-year-long war in Afghanistan. The Battle for Sangin in Helmand Province erupted in late 2010 when the Marine Corps took command control of the region from the Brits. 3rd Battalion, 5th Marines or "3/5," an infantry battalion out of Camp Pendleton California, were the main effort, and they were confronted with such a powerful and deeply entrenched opposing force that my infantry unit, Alpha Company from 1st Battalion, 23rd Marines was routed there to provide 3/5 support. As a part of that support, myself and twenty-six other Marines from 1/23 Alpha Company's 2nd Platoon were detached from our larger unit and designated as a mobile Quick Reaction Force for the region's main arterial mountain road, Route 611, running the 30-mile length of the lush Sangin river valley. We operated in a wide range of offensive and defensive capacities depending on the needs of any given day. Across the span of our time there we encountered near daily enemy entanglements, struck IEDs left and right, dealt death blows to nearly every enemy force that confronted us directly and we suffered tragic losses of our own.

The entire experience was extremely bolstering but it also tore holes in my inner man. War is taxing on the soul in ways not easy to imagine. Among other things there is a progressive abrasion that wears away the goodness in a person and leaves behind anger and hatred. What upheld me throughout and restrained what otherwise could have been a slide into complete moral relativism was my faith in a good God and experiential understanding of His intentional involvement in my life. I traversed through a dark and distress-filled valley but walked with God through it all. Now, years after climbing out the other side I look back on the challenging time in history and despite my personal costs I am thankful to have played a part in it.

As the years pass I think back on the war a lot less than I used to. For this book, however, I've thought deeply into all of it, re-engaging with every emotion again, and again. Many of my greatest personal triumphs and most bitter defeats are housed in memories of my life as a Marine. Some achievements and wounds alike imprint deep enough to leave lifelong marks and I carry many of both from that time of my life. I am a United States Marine and combat veteran. I served alongside some of America's finest men and women who chose to take a stand in defense of our nation and way of life, against

INTRODUCTION

the atrocities of a tyrannical enemy of terror. This is my story. There are many like it, but this one is mine.

> *'You cannot exaggerate about the Marines. They are convinced to the point of arrogance that they are the most ferocious fighters on earth and the amusing thing about it is that they are.'*[2]
>
> Chaplain Kevin Keaney

---

2. Mac Caltrider, *'The Most Ferocious Fighters on Earth' and Other Army and Navy Quotes about Marines.* (Coffee or Die Magazine, 2021), https://coffeeordie.com/finest-fighting-force-quotes

Chapter 1

IN THE BEGINNING

> *'I am convinced, that when we get to heaven, we'll find the streets are guarded by United States Marines.'*
> Ronald Reagan

Chaos. I learned to appreciate it. Situational instability in war gave room for more manic behaviors where I could let out my inner monster with diminished fear of consequence for overcompensation. The more chaotic the environment the freer I felt within it to escalate force with confidence and assertively kill my enemy as any good Marine would. In the context of war, killing the enemy is what my life and the lives of my fellow Marines centered on. It was the benchmark we gauged our self-worth and personal performance from and what we aspired to be absolutely excellent at. It didn't start that way though. It took a severe transformational process to produce a killer out of the lighthearted loving boy I was raised to be.

My war journey began on June 4, 2007, four days after my high school graduation. I said goodbye to everything I knew and boarded a nervous flight from Texas to southern California alone and with only the clothes on my back. After a short bus ride from the San Diego International Airport to the Marine Corps Recruit Depot, I stepped off the bus and claimed my place on the infamous yellow footprints that every Marine before me stood on and began my baptism into the brazen, cultish heritage of the United States Marine Corps. I was not there even a full twenty-four hours before feeling regret. I vividly remember a moment in the middle of the first night amidst the chaos of over-amped Drill Instructors domineering our massive herd of fresh recruits. Exhausted, and dumbfounded by my harsh new reality, the thought hit me, 'I could be enjoying myself poolside with my friends right now, holding my girlfriend and starting the best summer of my life. Instead, I volunteered myself into this rage-filled prison, which is only going to get worse and not let up for years. What was I thinking?'

For the next four days of the 'Processing Phase', my group of five hundred-plus, questionably motivated green recruits were taken to and fro across the Recruit Depot in humiliating fashion wearing our 'go fasters' (running shoes) and cammies buttoned all the way up the neck, which were the signifying markers of brand-new, 'First Phase', bottom of the barrel recruits among the thousands of others who were weeks ahead of us there. We went through rounds of medical and dental examinations, gear pickups, procedural briefings and more.

On the second day we were all taken to get vaccinations. As with every place we went, upon arrival we were lined up single file, standing, and crammed in as tightly together as we could get. 'NUT TO BUTT!' the Drill Instructors repeatedly screamed, and God forbid you did not comply. We shoved in waist to waist, eyes straight forward and mouths shut with no allowable deviation, baby stepping ahead as the line progressed, which took a couple hours. We went through a sort of assembly line consisting of seven Navy needle administrators, three on the left, three on the right and one at the end behind a curtain. When your position in the line came up you took a step forward and got two needles, one in each deltoid. Next step forward, two more needles, one in each deltoid again. Third step forward, two more needles, one in each triceps. If you were one of the few recruits that hadn't just fainted from receiving six injections in less than twenty seconds, you walked behind a curtain, pulled down your pants and bent over to receive the 'peanut butter' shot, which was a 4in x 1in vial of thick penicillin that was slowly injected into the butt cheek of their choice through a huge-gauge needle that resembled the size of a small electronics screwdriver. I was convinced the Navy Corpsman administering the peanut butter shot felt a demented enjoyment in how abruptly he stabbed the needle in and then how slowly and painfully he injected the thick fluid. It seemed all the corpsmen felt that way. We were undignified livestock to them, and they didn't refrain from asserting that. Upon completion, it was back into a line, nut to butt, eyes forward and mouths shut.

We attended administrative briefs, where we signed our lives away in stacks of contract paperwork, one of which included the assignment of beneficiaries for our fed gov 'SGLI' service members group life insurance policies should we be killed in training. Most of us eighteen-year-olds had never made a decision like that before. In the in-between times we were in the care and control of our Processing Drill Instructors, who had full rein over every aspect of our lives. There was never downtime, only Drill Instructor time. Sympathy in any form was completely non-existent and every human being we encountered in the Recruit Depot including chow hall staff, barbers, dental and medical personnel, office admin personnel, even facility maintenance staff treated us with intentional sub-human disdain, except the Drill Instructors, who treated us much worse.

In boot camp recruits are not prohibited to talk in first person. References to self are to be said as, 'This Recruit' and never 'I' or 'me'. Speaking with a Drill Instructor requires asking permission by screaming, 'THIS RECRUIT REQUESTS PERMISSION TO SPEAK TO DRILL INSTRUCTOR (insert name)!' Most requests were denied, and especially so if the request was missaid or said without the proper level of speed and intensity. There was nothing anyone could do to garner favor or positive reinforcement of any kind. No matter what you did or said about anything whatsoever, you were wrong, stupid, and usually punished for even trying. Freedoms of the smallest kind, like choosing when to use the restroom, or even to sit or stand at any moment, were prohibited. We were to do what we were told only, when we were told, and nothing more or less. Explicit obedience to every specific detail of every directive was the name of the game and it sucked.

On one occasion, after hours of being restricted from using the restroom, I struggled to walk because of intense bladder pain and began to fall behind while marching back to the squad bay from the chow hall. I had previously requested to use the head several times and was denied each time. With no other option, I let loose and urinated all over myself. When we got back to the squad bay and the Drill Instructor noticed what I did, I was punished for it with Intensive Training, better known by the acronym 'I.T.' I.T. in basic terms consisted of getting publicly smoke checked by a Drill Instructor for what felt like hours through a long, rage-filled episode of up-downs, push-ups, sit-ups, mountain climbers, and any other stationary calisthenics the Drill Instructors could come up with while they railed appalling profanities and insults at you, spit in your face, and ridiculed every aspect of your weak, pathetically worthless existence. The moment you showed any sign of fatigue they would come on even harder and dear God if you issued even a hint of complaint or showed any sign of emotional distress, other than unfiltered enragement, the suffering intensified immensely, often to the point that your body could literally take no more. After the savagery of my first I.T. punishment, I walked away like a beat dog with my tail tucked between my piss-and-sweat-covered legs. All the other recruits' eyes were square on me, and I felt so ashamed. It didn't really matter though. It was Processing Week and every ten minutes it seemed a new recruit was getting I.T.'d for something.

Opportunities to defecate came few and far between and when they did come, which was usually at the end of the day in the squad bay, there was no toilet paper, because the Drill Instructors prohibited its use. After realizing this on the first day, I stole napkins from the chow hall and hid them for eventual use to avoid the inevitable nastiness. When the time came, I was caught using them given there were no partitions around the toilets, and then I was punished again with I.T. for disobeying and stealing.

When the second night rolled around, the Drill Instructors had us cram into the Squad Bay restrooms to perform nightly hygiene. Because we did not respond to their order with enough haste, they lined us up shoulder to shoulder and instructed us to shave not our own face, but the recruit's face beside us, while the recruit on our other side shaved ours. Somewhat bewildered by the order, we commenced but lacked the right level of assertive action while performing the act, so the Drill Instructors ordered us immediately to put the razors down and pick up toothbrushes to brush the teeth of the recruit beside us while they ridiculed our lack of resolve. Still struggling to accept the abnormality of the situation, threats began to roll in of the many other more sinister hygiene group activities that imminently awaited us if we did not fix ourselves. This time the seriousness of the situation clicked, and we all immediately picked up the pace.

By the third night, the vaccinations had taken their hold on me, and my left arm and right butt cheek were in excruciating pain. Both were very swollen and flush red from adverse reactions. My right arm was not much better either, just not as raging bad as the other two. Even a small touch sent shudders of pain up and down my extremities. Because both sides of my body were in severe pain, I couldn't find any real relief laying down to sleep at night, which limited the already short amount of sleep they allowed us to have. Sometime after managing to fall asleep, I awoke suddenly from an abrupt burst of pain and quickly realized I had fallen out of my rack and landed on the cold unforgiving concrete floor. Exhausted, emotionally shocked, and in immense pain from the negative effects of seven simultaneous injections, I broke down in tears. I remember wanting just a little relief from it all but as I looked around the dark, quiet, prison-like squad bay I knew that there was no relief. I realized I was flagging myself as being weak and that, should I wake up other recruits or the Drill Instructors, the agony would be further amplified by more merciless punishment. In that moment it all clicked for me. My personal sovereignty was gone. If I was going to make it through, it was going to be on their program. I knew in that moment that I had to suck it up and accept it. I was already broken, and they managed to get me there that quickly, which is exactly the point of it all. Every one of us recruits showed up with an ego, confidence in our personal strengths, pride in our previous life achievements and the boast that we had willfully chosen to join the fiercest fighting force in the world; and during a time of war at that. None of those platforms of self-confidence would carry any real weight in the intensity of war though and they would all inhibit the developmental process of becoming a United States Marine. At the Marine Corps Recruit Depot, they pull out all the stops and rip out the foundation of a person so they can effectively build that person back up as a Marine. It is all a part of the process of indoctrination, and it works.

In the three months that followed I was physically and mentally pushed beyond any previous life experience. I was hardened quickly, and became laser focused on the execution of every order given to me. As the days progressed, so did my emotional callousness and full acceptance of my new family of violence, so much so that within a couple weeks I held one of only five leadership positions in my ninety-man platoon. Two weeks later I assumed the single highest position of Platoon Guide. This gave me closer proximity to my three Drill Instructors and demanded a much higher level of personal accountability and performance. For the remainder of boot camp I led my entire ninety-man platoon as the top recruit, took responsibility for their performance, bore direct punishment for their failures, and set a rigid example to be followed. By the time I graduated boot camp as Platoon Honorman of Lima Company Platoon 3242, I was completely bought in to MY Marine Corps. I felt bullet proof and was ready to charge into whatever hellish battlefield they sent me to.

SETTING THE DEPLOYMENT STAGE

Fast forward three years. It is October 1, 2010. As one of roughly 830 Marines (typical battalion size) in 1st Battalion, 23rd Marine Regiment, known as the 'Lone Star Battalion', I arrived at Camp Pendleton, California, beginning a pre-deployment work-up for combat in Afghanistan. We were on schedule to replace 3rd Battalion, 25th Marines, who were already there. I was in 2nd Platoon (40 Marines) of Alpha Company (165 Marines) out of Houston, Texas. We were a broad mix of individuals with various levels of life experience in and out of the military. Our most senior enlisted had numerous combat deployments under their belts and it showed. They were ruthless but pragmatic unit leaders marked by the reality of their wartime experiences in Iraq and they knew better than any of us what we were heading into. The war in Afghanistan was another animal though.

Afghanistan was and still is known as the graveyard of empires. For centuries warring groups have come and gone including even the likes of Alexander the Great and Genghis Khan, all leaving their marks but never completely conquering Afghanistan in any lasting way. In the more recent century, when outsiders weren't invading, Afghanistan's numerous tribes were in constant armed conflict with one another. The decades preceding our deployment were no different. Russia had invaded Afghanistan in 1979 during a period of civil war after the existing Afghan government had been internally overthrown. For ten years Russia tried to subdue the nation but to no avail. They pulled out in 1989 after their brutal war claimed the lives of 1.5 million Afghans[3] and the nation went right back into disarray. Tribal warlords filled in the power vacuum and contested one another for territorial control. It was during this period that various fringe groups like the Taliban and Al-Qaeda rooted in.

The story of the Taliban's upcoming tells like a hero's fable. After the Soviet–Afghan War, Afghanistan had no complete centralized government. The people of Afghanistan were largely left to fend for themselves under many third-world abuses. On once such occasion, a warlord was said to have kidnapped two teenage girls from a rural village and taken them to a military encampment as sex slaves for him and his men. This type of atrocity was not infrequent during that time but on this occasion a regional Mullah by the name of Mohammed Omar was compelled into action. Omar was approached by the family of the girls who were kidnapped, and he responded by recruiting thirty

---

3. Ahmed Rashid, *Taliban* (New Haven and London, Yale University Press, 2010), p.18.

of his students, in the local language of Pashto called 'Talibs', to launch an attack on the miliary encampment and free the young girls. His plan was executed successfully, and he liberated the girls from their captors, killing many of the opposing fighters including the enslaving warlord.[4]

Mullah Omar was a veteran and war hero of the Soviet–Afghan War. In a battle that claimed his fame, Omar was said to have organized a successful ambush on a Russian tank convoy in which he and a small band of combatants repelled the tanks' advance. Omar lost one of his eyes during the fight from shrapnel, which turned into a heralded war scar testifying of his warfighting dexterity. More than a fighter, Mohammed Omar was a pious man. Rather than advancing to seize power after the Soviets departed like many other Afghan war leaders, Omar retracted from the public eye and turned his focus to religious studies and instruction in one of Afghanistan's many madrasas (Islamic schools). During that time, he witnessed the abuses that were rampant in the nation and in the case of the two girls who were kidnapped Omar decided to take action.

After this occurrence, Mullah Omar and his followers seemed to explode across the country as they aggressed against other oppressors. They named themselves the Taliban, which means 'students' (of Islam), as a tether and identifier of their Islamic fundamentalism. They stood as liberators and protectors of the oppressed, but their altruism was highly tainted given their religious persuasions enacted severe repression of women, barbaric criminal justice practices and oppressive mandates upon the masses. They liberated people from other oppressors, only to enact their own form of tyrannical oppression right back on them.

In the same post-Russian war period, Al-Qaeda was expanding under Osama bin Laden, who was said to have initially come to Afghanistan to train and fight against the Soviets. Bin Laden came from wealth in Saudi Arabia and used that wealth throughout the late 1980s and early '90s to build up and establish Al-Qaeda, which was apparently founded around benefiting Saudi Soviet–Afghan war veterans and their families.[5]

---

4. Ibid., p.25.
5. Ibid., p.132.

Al-Qaeda's aim under bin Laden eventually shifted to global jihad, though, where nations that didn't align with his religious persuasions became enemies to terrorize and kill. After several terrorist bombings in the late '90s on US embassies and eventually a suicide bombing of the USS *Cole*, all of which killed Americans, the US Government began working toward eliminating bin Laden. Efforts became too little too late once the World Trade Center towers in New York were attacked on September 11, 2001. At this point, the Taliban had become a major power in Afghanistan and the Al-Qaeda leadership, including bin Laden, enjoyed the Taliban's protection and safe harbor from within the warlord nation. Ultimatums were issued to Mullah Omar to turn over bin Laden to the United States and, upon his rejection, the war drums sounded.

I was in seventh grade on September 11, 2001, when the World Trade Center Twin Towers fell. I remember watching the second plane hit the second tower live on a small box television in my gym class coach's office. At thirteen years old I was shocked at witnessing the event. In the years that followed, I watched broadcast after broadcast on the evening news of US troops in combat and had a distant discovery of the brutality of war. I remember the early air bombing campaigns in Afghanistan in 2002, the invasion of Iraq in 2003 and all the destruction that accompanied both. I remember seeing images of the mutilated bodies of two Blackwater contractors hanging from the now infamous green metal bridge in Fallujah in 2004. I tuned into news reports almost every evening during Operation Phantom Fury in November of that same year as Marines fought hellaciously door to door for control of Fallujah, sustaining bitter casualties but advancing through them. I was deeply impacted by it all. There was justice in our retribution and a resounding meaningfulness in our military's efforts to snuff out every flicker of terrorism that had for years taken violent actions against Americans. It was all in defense of freedom and toward the goal of re-establishing peace and security. There was also such goodness in the liberation of masses of people who lived under the tyrannical oppression of the Taliban, Saddam Hussein and other would-be authoritarian regimes. Both Operation Iraqi

Freedom and Operation Enduring Freedom in Afghanistan were causes that resonated with me for all the right reasons at the time.

I knew very well throughout my childhood the privilege of being born an American and experiencing the everyday individual freedoms that so many around the world had never known. I cannot remember a time I ever really questioned whether I wanted to serve in America's military. I always felt it was my duty to do so. I wanted to make my life matter and be a contributing part of something bigger and more important than myself. I wanted to serve my country and protect my home and the people I loved. By the time I was old enough to sign my Marine Corps contract, I was fully convinced. The pervasive evil of tyranny and terror was on full display and spreading throughout the world. After several years already of the Global War on Terror, it was my time to act. At my coming of age, I was not going to be a young man who chose to sit on the sideline and let others deal with the situation. I was determined to get involved and become a defender of my nation, a liberator of the oppressed, and a peacemaker in our conflict-stricken world. I believed I could make a difference and like so many others I risked everything to act on that belief.

America was founded on the idea of men and women living free of other's oppression. That freedom has been fought for, bled for and greatly sacrificed for from one generation to the next. I am confident that the privilege of living as a free person in a free and just society will always have to be fought for because there will always be those who selfishly endeavor to seize power for themselves and establish oppressive control over other people. It will forever be the burden of good men and women to stand in defense of freedom and at times war against those who attempt to squelch it, lest those good men and women accept a more dismal existence under the tyranny of others.

> *'The tree of liberty must be refreshed from time to time with the blood of patriots and tyrants.'*
>
> Thomas Jefferson

Chapter 2

INTO THE CAULDRON

'And I heard the voice of the Lord saying, "Whom shall I send? Who will go for us?" and I said, "Here am I Lord, send me.'

Isaiah 6:8

The start of our five-month pre-deployment work-up at Camp Pendleton in southern California was a mix of training and education. 2nd Platoon collectively bought a number of books on Afghanistan history, wartime tactics from the Soviet–Afghan War, and other relevant topics. We dove into the information alongside the Marine Corps programed educational courses as we sought to gain understanding of the dynamics that undergirded our enemy. Our training took off and we were in and out of the field constantly. The first field op we completed consisted of eight different live-fire ranges involving target acquisition, movement to fire, maneuvering on enemy positions during the day and IR (infrared) target designation shoots at night. We spent five days expending thousands upon thousands of rounds sharpening our basic combat rifle skills. IED (Improvised Explosive Device) 'lane training' followed right behind, which was a big focus throughout the entire work-up given IEDs were a major killer in Afghanistan. We ran security patrols in pre-staged areas that were set up with mock IED surprise attacks and machine gun ambushes. We were taught the various ways that IEDs were constructed, the enemy strategies behind their specific implementations, what IED indicators to look for while patrolling, SOPs (Standard Operating Procedures) for IED disarmament/disposal, and more.

IEDs were held in two categories, which were anti-personnel and anti-vehicle. Their construction was generally similar, but the volume of ammonium nitrate and the amount of metal additives acting as shrapnel varied depending on their intended target. We referred to the anti-personnel IEDs most often as 'pressure plates', given they were often designed like landmines to explode by being stepped on. Their mechanism required downward 'pressure', enabling two electrical leads to connect that would set off a blasting cap, which would ignite a measured amount of ammonium nitrate and send the recipient of the blast for the ride of their life.

We jumped right into Combat Life Saver training, encompassing the various battlefield injuries and how to properly address them. Gunshot and shrapnel wounds are treated in various ways depending on what part of the body is hit. The first intended outcome of addressing wounds on the battlefield is to stop or slow blood loss. If that can be accomplished and a medevac (medical evacuation) scrambled soon enough after, the injured Marine has a much higher chance for survival, unless a major organ took a direct hit. Because of the pressure plate threat, we all carried four or more tourniquets on our gear and at specific, various locations on our bodies that could be reached with either hand in the event the other one was blown off. Self-aid is the first lifesaver in a battle given it may be minutes (all it takes for a bleed out) or longer before another Marine or Corpsman can get to the wounded under fire. If bodily shock is not too intense after a Marine is shot or has their extremities blown off from an IED, that Marine is to rip tourniquets from his gear and self-apply them as fast and tight as possible. It sounds crazy that a person could function sufficiently enough to apply tourniquets to themselves right after having body parts severed off, but Marines had proven it achievable already on the battlefield and as such it became a part of our standard training SOPs (Standard Operating Procedures). After all, a major arterial bleed can take less than a minute before it is too late.

Training intensified as the weeks progressed. We packed on more gear, carried more ammo, went longer distances, and engaged in increasingly more complex operational scenarios. Everything escalated. We would regularly perform things like a 5-mile hump with 75% full gear (100lb+) followed by combat patrols all day in the mountains, which often proved worse than the humps, and finish the day with NVG (Night Vision Goggles) patrols in the middle of the night, capturing only a few hours of sleep before the next day's regimen began. Intermixed with it all was classroom education on topics like Afghan culture, Middle East tribalism, societal authority hierarchy, customs and courtesies, family dynamics, etc. We were taught the basic tenets of Pashto, which is the dominant language in southern Afghanistan, and commonly used phrases such as 'Hello/Goodbye', 'Thank you', as well as 'Where are the bombs?' 'Drop your weapons', and 'Stop or I will shoot you'. We brushed up on 'Call for Fire' radio sequencing, land navigation principles, patrolling and various types and purposes thereof, ambushes and the proper implementation of various ambush types, and more.

We gradually narrowed our focus toward the specific dynamics of the battle space we were heading into real time. Intel from the unit we were going to replace, 3rd Battalion, 25th Marines, or 3/25, and others in their vicinity made it to us every few days and our training adjusted accordingly. In late October, we had a couple of Marines from another infantry unit that had just returned to Pendleton from southern Afghanistan visit our platoon and walk us through their recent experiences in Helmand Province. Helmand was home to the Pashtun tribe, which was the Taliban's predominant ethnic group. The province was all around very hostile to westerners. I remember taking specific notice of how rough the two Marines were. They were both very monotone, glazed over and rigid. I realized I was staring at what would be me a year ahead and I was very taken back as I quietly pondered on what they must have been through to make them both so shockingly weathered. They told us that pressure plates were EVERYWHERE and that we should expect well-planned and organized ambushes from Taliban, Iranian, and Pakistani military-trained insurgents that would attack in anywhere from fire team to company-sized elements. A fire team is a four-man team but a company could be up to fifty, which is no small enemy force. Also, Iranians and Pakistanis? We'd been told this before, but their validation still came as a surprise. They said that the enemy fighters were extremely cunning and adaptive. They knew how we liked to fight, and they exploited our tactics wherever they could. The amount of gear and ammo these guys advised us to take even on routine patrols was nearly double what we had been carrying at that point in training, which was already stressing our mobility limits. They insisted that at times death in the platoon was entirely random and that knowing the roles up and down the patrol element would be critical. Radio, Corpsman, machine gunner, point man, grenadier, etc., anyone at any point could take a round in the face and it was incumbent upon all of us to be able to pick up the slack in an instant when it occurred. This is a point that SSgt (Staff Sergeant) Smith, our Platoon Sergeant (positional title, second in command behind Platoon Commander) in 2nd Platoon, asserted regularly, and we all took it to heart. We closed out discussion with the two Marines and as I shook their hands, they both looked me right in the eyes, brother to brother, and issued their goodbyes. 'Good luck boys, stay sharp,' one of them said as they turned to walk out of the squad bay. We talked among ourselves after they left and reaffirmed all they asserted. It was becoming more real now, we could all feel it.

SPIRITUAL IMPACT

My reputation as a Christian made its way around my Battalion early in the work-up. I began the deployment determined to maintain my faith in highest regard. 'Eat and drink for tomorrow we die' is the reigning mentality of Marines. We work hard, fight hard, play hard and die hard. The cascaded severity of life in general yields limited lifestyle restraint in the ranks and getting caught up in it all is much easier than avoiding it. I knew the cards were stacked against me when our work-up started but I had committed myself to Jesus and as much as could stand it, I was going be bold about my faith, stay true to my convictions and be a light in the dark places we were headed into. I determined that as much as I would be a vocal witness, I would show the love of God by my actions even more. No one was going to out-serve me in the platoon. For a time I volunteered for almost every working party, belligerently held a positive attitude, and put others first any way I could as often as I could force myself to. I rallied the Marines who resided on the social peripherals into friendship, I positioned myself to help those who struggled, and I ate my pride again and again when it reared its ugly face. No one is without error, and I certainly wasn't either, but I really gave it my all. Time and again, I was ridiculed, lashed out at, slandered and discounted, but overtime my immovability became respected and before long Marines sought me out to confide in me, pray with me, discuss questions about God and share their spiritual experiences. Little by little I began to see the Lord work in other Marines' lives in connection to my effort. I lived out my faith with intentionality and answered honestly when asked about it. I believed if I would just be faithful with little, the Lord would amplify the effect and He did not disappoint.

Marine Corps culture doesn't allow for weakness; physical, mental, or spiritual, and devotion to any religious persuasion, especially Christianity, is often seen as weakness. After breaking through that fallacy in our unit, there came a widespread sense of boldness to be real about faith in God and many Christians who would not otherwise be suspected stepped forward to assert their belief and reliance in Jesus. One of the biggest life lessons I learned through the experience was that people respect you far more when you stand firm in something through periods of ridicule than if you bend to their opposing pressure. It is as if we intentionally test each other's sincerity through opposition to see if whatever it is we are supposedly standing up for is genuine. Even some of the Marines that hated my way of life respected me for standing firm in it over time. I just knew that God had in mind to prove himself to some of the toughest men I had ever encountered, and my faith grew exponentially when I watched Him do it. Galatians 6:9 says, 'Let us not become weary in doing good, for at the proper time we will reap a harvest if we do not give up.' I deeply believed that biblical promise and then watched it unfold time and again.

Of all the Marines I had an impact on during the work-up there may have been none more so than LCpl (Lance Corporal) Turner. Turner was as country boy as anyone I had ever met. He had a sincere heart, was hilarious in his backcountry way and garnered the love of our platoon. Something awe-inspiring happened to Turner in mid-October. In spring 2010, less than a year before our work-up began, Turner was hospitalized with MRSA Staph Infection in his leg. He was in the hospital for two weeks and off work for a month as the infection entered his bloodstream and spread through his body. He eventually recovered from the incident, but the infection came back in October during our work-up and rapidly worsened every day. It started as a football-sized blemish on his leg, but quickly spread, inflaming his whole leg and turning it bright red. I began praying for him and recruited people back home to do the same. Turner went to the on-base hospital on a Friday and received heavy medication. After spending the day there, he was returned to our Platoon on bed rest. The doctors had the Corpsman monitor his leg closely and asserted that if his condition worsened even a little, he would need to be back in the hospital asap. They even told Turner that it was not entirely unlikely under worst case scenario that he could lose his leg if the infection's spread was not quickly curbed, especially this being a reoccurrence. MRSA often beats the drugs given to fight it and this being a reoccurrence meant the infection hit harder and faster than before. By the end of day Saturday, Turner was much worse. His whole body started to swell and turn red. He looked and felt awful and started becoming very loopy. As it became obvious that he was in really bad shape, I went with Turner back to the Corpsman's squad bay, and they put in an immediate call for a vehicle to rush him back to the hospital. At that moment, I sent out word again to all the people I knew that would pray for him. A pastor back home even halted a Saturday night church service that was under way at that moment and had the entire congregation pray for Turner. I went outside with Turner while his ride was on the way to pick him up and we prayed together one more time, laying hands on him and asking God to heal him. The van showed up and I went back to the squad bay.

I updated those back home with the situation and urged them to continue praying. I also continued praying for Turner throughout the evening and eventually went to sleep. At 0100 I was suddenly shaken awake by TURNER ... Completely confused, I asked, 'Why are you not at the hospital?' He was all smiles, full of energy and his skin tone seemed back to normal. I was SHOCKED ... 'Turner, what happened?' I asked, now wide awake and with elevated concern. Turner proceeded to tell me that when he got to the hospital, he was lying in a triage bed and saw another patient in bad condition. He said that he felt compassion for that person and began to pray, 'Father, please heal them in Jesus' name. Whether or not I get healed of this infection please take care of them and heal them.' When he prayed, he said he felt the presence of God come on him so strong and instantly his infection began to subside. By the time he got before the doctors his condition had improved so significantly that they were dumbfounded and didn't know what to say about it. Checking his vitals, doing blood work, and monitoring Turner closely, they all watched his condition improve unexplainably fast, and eventually found no reason to keep him there overnight. By the next morning, Turner's leg had only a slight discoloration on it. Two days later, he was approved to return to full duty training.

In just a matter of days, Turner's infection had begun to spread throughout his body, becoming potentially life threatening and in what seemed like just a moment, it all dissipated. The longer I pondered on the whole thing in the following days the more blown away I became. How could something so bad just fade away so quickly? I praise God still to this day for the incredible work and for showing up in such a time of need. Previously Turner had wondered and been frustrated over not having had what he considered a real encounter with God. I think this experience profoundly addressed that.

> *'The prayer offered in faith will make the sick person well, and the Lord will raise them up.'*
>
> James 5:15

PUT ON NOTICE

From the start of our work-up through the end of October, our intended AO (Area of Operation) in Afghanistan was to be a place called Delaram in the Farah Province, which resided roughly one hundred miles east of the Iranian border. Our mission would be to uproot the Taliban's foothold in the region and enact a 'Drug Interdiction' mission to diminish the Taliban's heroin operation, as if planned to be intentionally ironic given we were a Texas unit where drug trade on the border with Mexico was so rampant. We were told that 70% of the world's heroin of that day originated in southern Afghanistan farmlands. The plant of origin was the beautiful, waist-tall, flowering 'poppy' and it grew very well in Afghanistan's arid climate. Poppy plants have golf ball-sized bulbs at the base of their vibrant flower petals and, when ripe, raw opium is extracted from those bulbs.

The global opium trade was connected to the localized Afghan economies[6] and the Taliban exploited it to their benefit, creating so

---

6. Ibid., p.118.

much revenue that it made up roughly 50% of their annual funding at the time. The Taliban would transport the opium out of Afghanistan into Iran, Pakistan, and other surrounding countries, where it would be refined into heroin and distributed to the world. If we crippled that revenue stream, it would be a big hit to the Taliban's economic strength. Because Delaram was one of the largest townships on a major highway near the Iranian border, it was very strategically important to the Taliban's export operation.

At the start of November, a major shift happened. We received word that Delaram was being put on the back burner for Alpha Company and our mission focus was changing. Over the month of October in 2010, a large-scale Marine Corps mission began in a highly strategic region of the Helmand Province called Sangin. Sangin was a part of the vast agriculturally plush river valley that followed the mighty Helmand River, which snaked out of Afghanistan's northern mountains, through a township called Kajaki and then and flowed south. The area in focus spanned from several miles south of the Sangin urban epicenter all the way up to Kajaki, which was roughly a 30-mile densely populated mountainous stretch. This region had long been a major enemy stronghold given the significance of its locational and geographic characteristics. Sangin was an enormous opium producer and in 2010 it was one of the last of its size still in enemy control. In the preceding year, the Marine Corps had taken over command control of the entire Helmand Province, a major shift in the war, and was launching large-scale enemy-eradication operations in townships both north and south of the Sangin region, including Kajaki and Marjah in particular, which effectively pushed the enemy to regroup and dig into Sangin. In this regard, Sangin was reminiscent of Ramadi in Iraq after Marines pounded the insurgents out of Fallujah in 2004. It was primed to explode the moment the Marines stepped foot there.

For the preceding years, the Sangin region had operationally belonged to the Brits, who had a less aggressive peacekeeping focus with a limited footprint and concentration in the main urban epicenter. When the Marine Corps took command control of the region, the strategic intent shifted entirely to affirmative combat action. 3rd Battalion, 5th Marines was essentially tasked with sweeping the valley and eliminating enemy forces. Overnight, regional stability deteriorated and Sangin turned into the most kinetic combat operating zone in Afghanistan. 3/5 sustained ten KIAs (killed in action) and thirty-five additional WIA (wounded in action) in their first three days of operations in Sangin.[7] On October 23, they got hit with fifteen small arms attacks and eight IED strikes in one day, which was said to be an average day. By the end of their first month, they had sustained fifteen KIAs, more than forty amputees and over seventy WIA.[8] For Afghanistan, it did not get any worse than this. It was so bad that the US Secretary of Defense, Robert Gates, apparently tried to pull the Marines out of the region entirely, as had recently been done to an Army unit that suffered extreme opposition in the Korengal Valley famed by the documentary *The Hornets' Nest*. The Commandant of the Marine Corps doubled down against that move, however, asserting that Marines don't run from fights, and he was unwaveringly certain that the Marines would be the last men standing in Sangin.[9] Given the extreme severity of enemy resistance that 3/5 was encountering, 3/25, the unit we would replace, was re-tasked from Delaram to Sangin to reinforce 3/5, which also sealed our fate to the region.

Stabilizing Sangin was a very complex challenge. Opium farming was done by the civilian 'local nationals', who grew and harvested it and then sold their crop to the Taliban. This meant we couldn't just wipe out all the fields or we'd pit the locals against us. Instead, we had to remove the Taliban before the exchange could happen while

---

7. Bing West, *One Million Steps: A Marine Platoon at War* (New York: Random House, 2014), p.23.
8. Ibid., p.70.
9. Ibid., p.71.

introducing new regional infrastructure and economic opportunities to lessen the blow to the local economy. It was messy. At the upper level of our regional strategy resided a plan to improve and increase energy turbines at the Kajaki dam 30 miles north of Sangin to supply the region with improved power. This required the main roadway up and down the valley, Route 611, to be opened and completely controlled by US forces. The further north that the 3/5 Marines ventured on the 611 toward that goal, however, the more perilous it became as battle after battle ensued.

In Sangin there was said to be numerous reigning Taliban cells with hundreds of troops each at any given time that consistently ambushed our patrols, our LPs/OPs (Listening Posts/Observation Posts) and FOBs (Forward Operating Bases). That number grew in mass in the spring and summer during 'fighting season' as foreign insurgency fighters traveled in from other countries. Many of the fighters were properly military trained with combat experience and were putting together well-coordinated attacks and ambushes, just like the two recently returned Marines had shared with us weeks prior. We were told that one October ambush on a 3/5 foot patrol would have resulted in a total decimation of the Marines if it had not been for air support, which says a lot. The situation was heavy and escalating, and our deployment schedule of early spring 2011 put us on the ground right at the beginning of the next fighting season.

General John Kelly, the Commanding General of the 4th Marine Division at the time, came to speak to our Battalion in person about our upcoming deployment just days after we received word that Sangin was our new destination. His son was coincidentally a Platoon Commander with 3/5 in Sangin at the time. He spoke at length about the strategic importance of the region, the mounting casualties given the ferocity of the enemy fighters there and their determination to hold it, and the dynamics of the combat operations we were soon to be engulfed in. He said that Sangin was in that day one of the last major Taliban strongholds in Afghanistan and that they would fight to the death to retain it. He wished us luck and assured us that the eyes of the Marine Corps and of the nation would soon to be upon us. It was extremely bolstering. On November 9, 2010, just one day after General Kelly came to speak to us, his son, 1st Lt Robert Kelly was killed in action in Sangin. It seemed surreal when I heard it. General Kelly was so optimistic and resolute in his speech about Sangin and one day later was dealt the most crippling blow with the loss of his own son in that same battlespace. If anything, this put a postmark confirmation on all that we'd heard. We were about to be a part of a major operation that could result in a large-scale shift in the entire Afghanistan conflict, and it was sure to be as bad as we had been told.

At this point in time, we were not ready for the challenges we would soon face. Some of the Marines were nervous and others were mentally unprepared, but we collectively determined that by the end of our work-up we would be ready and that any who were not would be uninvited to the party. Our mentality started becoming more rigid and our training intensity shifted in severity once again. 2nd Platoon in particular took on a new fervor. The seemingly unknown was now taking shape and forefront in all our minds were the battles ahead. We were undergoing the mental shifts necessary to persevere in war as we increasingly came in tune with the inevitable trials that awaited us.

PROMOTION

In mid-December we spent numerous cold and wet days in the field going through a squad-sized live-fire range, more IED scenarios, MOUT training (Marine Operations in Urban Terrain) and more. During one training evolution we practiced battlefield casevac (casualty evacuation) procedures with two Chinook helicopters that were running through mock operations with us. We called in 9-line casualty evacuation requests to our COC (Command Operations Center), who then paired us over to the Chinook pilots to give landing zone briefs to directly. A "9-line" is a standardized radio report format used to communicate critical information associated with casevac requests. The helos would land, and we loaded onto them for a quick dust off and flight around the area while the next Marine hopped on the radio to do the same thing. We rolled into night missions right after casevac training and ended the day in our sleeping bags after midnight. I was awakened at 0300 (am) for fire watch, which is one of the worst shifts. Very tired and still sopping wet from the night patrols, I got up, put my boots and jacket on and took watch for the next hour in the cold. It was all I could do to stay warm and awake, and I paced around the perimeter of all the sleeping Marines with my rifle slung over my shoulder and prayed the hour away while looking up at the most amazing display of stars. My whole life I have been enamored by the stars at night. For all that we think we know and concern ourselves with here in our day to day there is profoundly more out there than we remember to bear in mind. The longer I looked at the stars and confided in the Lord, the less concerned I was about the cold or my fatigue. Throughout the entire deployment, time alone with God was regularly a sustaining grace for me and I did everything I could to capture moments like this when chances arose.

We woke up at 0530 the next morning and went into Entry Choke Point (ECP) training, setting up barricades and concertina wire and rehearsed procedures. An ECP disallows vehicles from steamrolling through a gate. A common suicide bomb tactic in Iraq was barreling a V-BIED (Vehicle-Born IED) through our base entries and setting off, which often caused mass casualties. An ECP prevents a vehicle from being able to get close to the main entry at speed and allows plenty of time for Marines guarding the entry to kill the driver and stop the vehicle if they do not comply. We jumped from ECP training to more vehicle patrolling and finally returned to the squad bay from the field late that night. After cleaning our weapons and taking care of our gear, we went to sleep. Four hours later we geared back up to set out on a 9-mile hump, during which I foolishly chose to wear my new boots that were only partially broken in and my feet paid the price. I had coin-sized blisters on my feet when we got back, which made for great fun in the days following as the training tempo didn't slow down any. We kept up this around-the-clock pace into the new year, jamming in as much training as possible as our time for departure neared.

With the turn of the year came my promotion to Corporal (Cpl), a huge accomplishment for a young Marine and especially in the infantry. Corporal is the first noncommissioned officer (NCO) rank and it came with new leadership opportunities and elevated unit responsibilities. We went up to Range 800, which resides atop one of the tallest mountain ranges on Camp Pendleton. The weather was cold and rainy, but it was beautiful. Rolling hills of bright green grass extended in every direction. Several mornings, we woke up to picturesque sunrises and we ended each day's training to beautiful sunsets. We ran through squad-sized live-fire assaults on a mock town with 'imbedded enemy troops'. The assaults began with coordinated mortars, machine gun and sniper fire, while the main assault element attacked the 'objective' directly. It was the first time in the work-up that we integrated all parts of the infantry in coordinated operation with one another in live-fire assaults and it was an awesome experience.

My promotion ceremony was held out there in the field. With all the platoons formed up, raggedy and muddy from long field training days, I marched in front of our Alpha Company Commanding Officer and Company Gunnery Sergeant to get pinned my new chevrons. I was filled with gratitude and praised God for this sought after promotion. When the ceremony ended my platoon came to congratulate me. 'You deserve this more than anyone,' one of them said, which meant more to me than any other affirmation. From the start of the work-up I determined to serve the platoon, to be humble and to have an attitude of gratitude regardless of my circumstances. I didn't walk this out with perfection but really endeavored to and I think this played a big part in my promotion. Following the pinning ceremony was the most beautiful sunset all the way out over the ocean and far past the horizon over the cities in the distance. I reveled in the moment and thanked God for all he had carried me through up to that point. It was one of the best moments of my life and one I'll never forget.

> *'Everyone who exalts himself will be humbled, but he who humbles himself will be exalted.'*
>
> Matthew 23:12

AGGRESSIVE TRAINING TEMPO

Throughout the work-up we received frequent updates from units in Sangin as their knowledge of the region expanded. Among all topics of information provided, one of the more challenging to grasp was Sangin's sociocultural dynamics. Tribal male hierarchy was the mainstay power structure and elders especially carried the weight of rulership. Obviously, we endeavored to win over key elders throughout the region, but they were found regularly to be serving both sides of the conflict despite our constant efforts. The governing mentality of those in power was evidently self-serving, and their loyalties often resided with whoever best served their personal interests of any given day. Principles didn't guide decision-making for them, self-benefit did. Further complicating things were family networks. Committed enemy combatants were often sons, nephews, brothers, or cousins to the elders that we were propositioning. Taliban leadership was also intertwined with regional hierarchies like the Mob and alliances were all blurred. Foreign insurgents added another layer of convolution. They traveled into Afghanistan from any number of outside countries and operated both autonomously and integrated within the Taliban units. They forced their influence on the local population through fear and coercion and were supplied often through out of country back channels and local seizure of others' belongings.

Little about our enemy was black and white, creating difficulty in determining exactly how to combat them. We Marines were brought up through foundational training for conventional armed conflict where overwhelming force and aggressive violence wins the day, but the war in Afghanistan was far from conventional. We had no problem going toe to toe with a squared up enemy force but fighting against guerrilla tactics undergirded by a value system that was foreign to our western world mentality was a very different challenge. We were to think like Marines and not like Marines at the same time, which made for a world of frustration in strategic planning.

In mid-January our training tempo peaked. It was high stakes now as we pulled together all the previous months' work into our broadened operational training exercises. Within the Battalion, at the Company and Platoon level especially, we were competing to outperform one another. Top performers got tasked with the high-speed missions in theatre and no one was collectively more determined to secure those missions than we were in 2nd Platoon.

There were three final events to undergo and the first was Camp Pendleton's 'Infantry Immersion Range', which was a completely built and furnished mock Afghanistan town including a multitude of Afghani actors that played every role to be expected of a real-time Afghan community. The intent was to simulate what it would be like getting ambushed while patrolling through an actual Afghan town on an average day. When I say Afghani actors, I mean actual Afghanistan national citizens that were in the US on work visas with the Department of Defense specifically to aid our training for deployments. Taxpayer dollars at work. We received six different missions over three days, such as finding and speaking with the local Mullah, routine security foot patrols to various checkpoints, raiding suspected insurgent-held compounds in the middle of the night and more. There was an OPFOR (Opposing Force) comprised of Marines from another Camp Pendleton unit unaffiliated to ours who were specifically trained to fight like insurgents. They were intertwined through the range and were launching ambushes on us in every mission. They were shooting at us with actual paintball projectiles, and we returned fire with the same. When any of us got hit, it was treated like actual casualties, meaning we had to drag each other out of the kill zones, administer aid while fending off our attackers, coordinate casevacs (casualty evacuations), call in 9-lines, pivot to patrol contingencies, etc. It felt real, very real, so much so that at one point I got into it with one of the Afghani actors and I couldn't tell whether he was in actor mode or not. What I saw was a potential insurgent charging me up slinging threats in my face. As he refused to back off at my intensified orders,

I became enraged and smashed my rifle barrel into his chest, shoving him back. I squared up to hit him again even harder and the training instructor quickly grabbed me by my chest rig, ripped me back and sent me off the course. I was HEATED, but after calming down I realized with a convoluted self-satisfaction that my aggression level was gaining range. The whole episode was extremely frustrating but affirming given the context. All my mental preparation to actually act out in real, unfiltered physical force was working.

One of the more difficult dichotomies of being a Marine in training is having to maintain a heightened potential for actionable violence but restraining that potential with no real, non-training outlet. It often felt like being a caged fighting dog, prodded and antagonized into fury but kept confined and unable to act out on the built-up aggression. Other times it was difficult to take seriously at all because the reality of actual warfighting in training is ultimately imaginary with no one shooting back. I think this conflicted mental positioning is one of the things that creates real struggle for Marines when they leave the service, and especially if they never got the chance to participate in actual battle. Imagine dedicating years of your life to training for an athletic competition with the anticipation of someday getting the chance to compete for real, but ultimately never getting to. For me, even while fully aware of the likelihood of actual combat in the near future, controlling the heightened emotion in training was at times notably difficult. Being fully emotionally and physically ready for extreme violence but restraining myself from actually performing it day after day, month after month, etc. inflicted a very strange stress on me.

We completed the Infantry Immersion Range and moved back up the mountain to Range 600 for our final coordinated live-fire attacks of the work-up. Running through this range smoke checked me worse than any other. I was a fire team leader, had full gear on with all four sappy plates, three hundred-plus rounds of ammo, eighteen 203 training rounds, smoke grenades and an extra SAW (M249 Squad Automatic Weapon, belt-fed machine gun) ammo drum for my SAW gunner on the assaults. Like Range 800, we performed coordinated attacks on enemy positions but this time the attacks were platoon size. Mortars, snipers, heavy machine guns and rockets, including AT-4s (Anti-Tank shoulder fired rocket) and the SMAW, (Shoulder-launched Multipurpose Assault Weapon, also a shoulder fired rocket) kicked off the attack and our main body assault force followed. The amount of suppression by all the heavy weapons was very powerful. It was a blowout of rounds down range, fire and maneuver and advancing through enemy positions. It all felt great to execute live.

One of the craziest things happened in the middle of my second assault on Range 600. The range seemed to be roughly 500m long, and our main assault span was maybe 200 to 300m. Halfway through it, with all the added munitions weight I carried while sprinting, bounding, screaming, firing, etc., I was gassed. On one of my bounds midway through the assault, I jumped up, sprinted 20m or so and dropped down to begin firing again in typical fashion. This time though, on my way down I drove my left knee into a pointed boulder that was barely unearthed at its top. The stabbing pain was so severe that I rolled over on my side thinking I had just blown out my knee and ended my Marine Corps career before getting to deploy. While writhing in pain thinking the worst had just happened, one of the Range Safety Marines ran up to me and screamed, 'DON'T MOVE! THERE IS A HUGE RATTLE SNAKE RIGHT IN FRONT OF YOUR HEAD!' I couldn't hear him clearly the first time over all the surrounding gunfire, but he re-asserted from a safe distance, 'GIANT RADDLE SNAKE RIGHT BY YOUR FREAKING HEAD BRO!' I heard him that time for sure and in an instant the pain in my knee was dwarfed by a surge of fear and I exploded off the ground to get away while the Safety Marine began laughing hysterically. He wasn't kidding about the rattlesnake, just humorously surprised by my explosive fearful reaction. No way I was going to lay there and get bitten in the face by a rattler! Ha ha.

I limped through the end of the assault and inspected my knee when I got back at the staging area. It was a heavy blow, and I was really concerned I may have done lasting damage. There was another Marine in the work-up who had sustained a torn ACL just a few weeks prior and he got sent home for good. That was the absolute last thing I wanted. I babied my knee as much as I could in the following days and didn't dare get it checked out for fear that I could get yanked from the mission also. Thankfully strength came back in the following weeks but to this day my knee isn't right anymore.

We rolled into our FINEX (Final Exercise) right after Range 600, which was our last performance-assessed training evolution and final chance to prove our operational capabilities to the command hierarchy who would be a part of issuing our mission orders overseas. For several days, we underwent numerous mock operations involving an OPFOR (Opposing Force). We were housed in a compound simulating a FOB (Forward Operating Base) in a mountain valley. Upon arrival we fortified the compound, established sectors of fire, set up ECPs (Entry Choke Points), established response plans for attacks at various avenues of approach, posted fire watch schedules and security details, pre-staged numerous defensive positions, and much more. Throughout the four-day period we were 'attacked' day and night and responded accordingly. We had snipers embedded in the mountainside that enveloped our compound providing overwatch who would report incoming personnel, suspected enemy activity in any given direction and engage in our firefights from afar. Each day we went on mounted and dismounted patrols to given locations for various reasons, set up ambushes and repelled them. 2nd Platoon continued an aggressive pace. With mission tasking so near we did our best to stay focused. We put in long hours and held ourselves to rigid training standards. No one was more driven than we were and at the completion of the FINEX we were confident we had proven ourselves to be the best of our Battalion.

FINAL PREPARATIONS

In February I took one last trip home before leaving the States. I spent time with family and couldn't have hoped for a better final visit, but it was not easy. I spent the weekend reassuring my mother, who was already dealing with crippling worry. In my last goodbye with my grandmother, she hugged and kissed me, unable to control her tears. Grandad gave me a big hug and began to cry. A moment after letting go he turned back around, struggled to mutter my name, grabbed me by the neck and kissed me on the cheek while tears streamed down his cheeks. I had never seen my grandad cry before. This deployment would be a valley of shadows for us all in different ways and it hit me all too hard in that moment. Hours before driving me to the airport on my last morning home, my dad drove me to Veterans' Park, a place we frequented when I was a boy, and we went in his 1959 International Harvester pickup truck, which is the truck he and I would take on camping trips every year of my childhood. He wrote a detailed letter to read to me so he would not miss a word of all he had to say, as if it might be his last chance to really open up and talk to his only son face to face. Of all the things I remember about that moment, what impacted me the most was how vulnerable my dad was. All the years leading up to this his job was to be my provider and protector. Now his little boy was headed into a very dangerous place on his own far beyond the reach of Dad's protection. I cannot imagine how that felt. The events ahead were out of his control and all we could do was hope for the best, trusting that the Lord would be present and involved in whatever outcome.

My parents drove me to the airport later that morning in the gloomiest car ride I have ever been in. None of us knew what to say. When we pulled up to the airport entrance, we all got out for our final in-person embrace. Both parents hugged me tightly while we all fought back tears. When we let go and I turned to walk into the airport, the most bitter feeling hit me. I felt abandoned, like a child being ripped away from the love and protection of my parents. Mom and Dad later told me they sobbed all the way home, crushed by worry and pain. For many OEF (Operation Enduring Freedom) parents, experiences just like this were their last in-person encounters with their living, breathing children and the those that followed in the weeks and months after were reunions with only torn-up bodies encased in flag-draped caskets. This was in the forefront of mine' and my parents' minds as I'm sure it was in everyone else's.

Back at Pendleton we went into final preparations for our big departure. We celebrated all we had accomplished as all our major training evolutions were over. One late afternoon, just days before we departed, most of Alpha Company had an afternoon together on the beach. Gunnery Sergeant Coleman, aka "Gunny" huddled everyone up, gave a speech and got emotional. He said, 'I love every single one of y'all. Gents we're going to be hooking and jabbing over there. It is my job to get you all home and I don't know that I'll be able to do that on this one but I'm going to give my mother fucking all to make it happen.' Gunny Colemen was a Marine Corps icon, and his words carried more weight than anyone's in our company. He was a hard-charging Infantry Marine who fought in Charlie Company 1/8 in Desert Shield/Desert Storm, then engaged in combat in the Somalia conflict, which was famed by the movie *Black Hawk Down*, and he had been an active part of almost every major US armed conflict since. For the Global War on Terror, Gunny Coleman had three combat deployments to Iraq and two to Afghanistan. He also had been in just about every role in the Marine Corps Infantry, achieved the title 'Fittest Marine in the Marine Corps' by competition more than once, and was a MCMAP (Marine Corps Martial Arts Program) black belt with three red tabs. Barring all that, Gunny Coleman was huge, freakishly strong, dangerous, and among all men not one to be trifled with. There was not a man alive that any of us respected more and no one preferred anyone other than Coleman to be our Company Gunny on the deployment.

Celebrations aside, we spent a good amount of time getting our affairs in order. Consolidation of gear, shipping personal items home, buttoning up paperwork and going through final medical examinations was all the rage. Our most important focus though was tuning into the latest situational developments in Sangin. Days before our flight out of the US, one Marine General was cited in the *Marine Corps Times* newspaper saying, 'The mission of Sangin placed on 3/5 is as tough as any military operation in the History of the Marine Corps.'[10] It was a huge statement. 3/5 had suffered a significant number of casualties up to that point but not without effect. After the turn of the year, Marine forces in Sangin were said to have killed or captured more than six hundred enemy fighters[11] and the Marines of 3/5 were among the main contributors despite their losses. They certainly lived up to the Commandant's confidence when he refused to pull them out months prior at the suggestion of the Secretary of Defense.

From the time we were notified that our mission trajectory had shifted to Sangin, we were engrossed in details of 3/5's battle experiences and constantly reminded of the threats that awaited us. Now we were just days away from being boots on the ground and it was a nervous time, but we were Marines. After nearly five months of intense preparation specifically for this deployment, we were bullish and eager to hit it all head on. Every one of us volunteered ourselves into service while already in a time of war knowing that this may lie ahead. It is what I joined for. I wanted to be sent into the fray and do my part in our fight against the tyrants of my day. Carrying forward the legacy of generations of previous American warfighters, it was my time to stand in the gap and I wanted it no other way except that I would have already been there in the fight.

On the last day before our scheduled flight out of the US, SSgt (Staff Sergeant) Smith gathered many of us around the TV in our squad bay to give us a potent dose of reality. He played a handful of real, raw videos where insurgents had filmed themselves barbarically beheading their tied-up, helpless victims. I remember some of them in vivid detail and being both sobered and enraged. The hopeless

---

10. *Marine Corps* newspaper.
11. Jeffrey Dressler, *Counterinsurgency in Helmand: Progress and Remaining Challenges* (Washington DC, Institute for the Study of War, 2011).

pleas of some of the young victims and the sounds they made while their lives were mercilessly sawed away from them by their blood thirsty, maliciously evil captors struck a deep chord within me. It was easily the worst thing I had ever watched but I needed to see it. We had often talked through the potential outcomes of capture, and we all knew the risks. There would be no mercy given by our sadistic enemy and watching those videos removed any doubt. The brutal reality seared deeply into my mind and heart. I committed to myself right then that at any point should I wind up in a capture situation that I could not get out of I would forcibly fight to the death, *no matter what*. Kill them all, force them to kill me or I would kill myself, but I would never be captured alive. No matter what.

Later that day, we reviewed our final orders contracts, signed our Uncle Sam-issued life insurance policies awarding $400,000 dollars to the lucky recipients we chose should we be killed, and started making all our last calls home before leaving the homeland. The mood was complicated. I don't think there is a better word to describe it than that.

Chapter 3

THE BIG SHOW

'Tis not where we lie, but whence we fell; the loss of heaven is the greatest pain in hell.'
                                        Pedro Calderon de la Barca

My first impression of Afghanistan when I stepped off the monstrous C-17 that transported us there was anticlimactic. Everything appeared to be exactly what I had expected for a Third World country. It was March 1, 2011. We flew on a chartered plane from California to Maine, then to Ireland, and then to a staging base called Manas in Kyrgyzstan at the foothills of the Tian Shan Mountains, which towered over everything in view with massive snow-capped peaks on display. It was -1° when we arrived at Manas and -13° when we left. Afghanistan was warmer but not by much. We arrived at Kandahar from Manas, which was an unplanned stop on our way to Camp Leatherneck. In just hours after arriving at Kandahar a triple amputee and two other wounded Army soldiers were flown in and went straight into a trauma center that we happen to be staged right beside. Our Corpsmen went inside to help. After thirty minutes Doc Sisley exited the trauma building and told us what was going on. He was visibly distraught. The triple amputee had just bled out on the operating table. One of the others had also just succumbed to his injuries and the doctors were still feverishly trying to stabilize the third, but it didn't look good for him either. One of our Marines made a crass joke about it all and Sisley twisted off at him in anger and disgust. I didn't know what to think. This was our first real encounter with combat death, which we all tried to treat laughably as a coping mechanism prior to this experience but it was different now. I felt deeply saddened for those soldiers, their unit and their families who would soon be receiving the news that all our families feared most. There was no sugar coating anything after that experience. We were in it, and it was all real.

Our advanced party was already in Sangin at FOB Jackson, one of the only three sizable friendly military establishments in that region. They were being attacked daily at the FOB. The insurgents were even getting close enough to drop grenades into the perimeter posts, which was reminiscent of the Soviet–Afghan War. One of the Mujahadeen's fear tactics with the Russians was to sneak up on perimeter security posts at night, capture and decapitate the soldier standing guard and leave his headless remains to be found the following morning by his comrades to inflict fear. We were warned to be mindful of their attempts to do the same thing to us.

Night rolled around and we geared up, broke into smaller groups, and loaded onto C-130s for a short flight to Camp Leatherneck under the cover of darkness. As we waited for the C-130s to arrive for our pickup we ran into a group of military surgeons on the flight line who were on their way home. One of them said that in the seven months he had been there he came across twenty-three triple amputees, and twice as many singles and doubles, not counting the multitude of gunshot and shrapnel wounds. Another surgeon said he came across eighty-six amputees total and that 95% of them lost their genitals. That is exactly what we didn't want to hear. They warned us to tread carefully, and we took it to heart.

We landed at Leatherneck before sunrise and immediately began receiving all our introductory briefs. The first was on IEDs. Most of the information was not new to us at that point, but things were changing daily, it seemed. Of all the differences between the insurgents' tactics in Iraq and those deployed in Afghanistan, none were more impressive than their IED engineering. I was blown away (pun intended) at how many different configurations of actual found and defused IEDs we were shown. There were twenty-plus laid out on a table for us to study. Pressure plates; trip wires; remote detonation; hard-wire, push-button detonate; pull-string detonate; magnetic detonate; directional blast; bated traps; anti-tamper devices; false-deactivation wires; and on and on and on. They would tie strings to pieces of our gear for us to find and pick up and an IED would detonate when we did. If we threw out dead batteries, there was still enough charge to be used for a detonation. They even developed IEDs with no detectable metal content so our metal detectors would not pick them up as we started to walk across them. One method of our EOD (Explosive Ordnance Disposal) teams was to finger through disturbed earth patches (recently dug and refilled holes) to try to gently locate the edge of an IED's mechanism so as to identify where to place C4 to neutralize it. The Taliban took notice and started making IEDs with loose strings of wire that resembled the neck of a guitar, so that as an EOD Marine gently fingered through the dirt, they would ever so slightly drag or push one wire string into touching another, closing the electrical circuit and setting the IED off in their face. The enemy's inventive creativity with both their IED design and deployment was creditworthy for sure and we were starkly warned not to underestimate either. The IEDs were becoming more undetectable and were said to be littered throughout the more contested AOs (Area of Operation). We were advised to get used to adapting our patrolling and fighting tactics continuously throughout the coming months as the enemy was rapidly adapting theirs.

The next few briefs were reminders of the overarching COIN (Counter Insurgency) Mission, the specific COIN initiatives of that day, the geographic outlay of friendly forces, both operational and static, and then a brief on standard procedures if captured. That issue was already settled with many of us, and all the brief did was reaffirm our position on it.

Our final brief was on ROEs (Rules of Engagement), which procedurally took place right before we were handed a massive amount of ammunition. It was presented by a well-rehearsed Judge Advocate General (JAG) attorney, who would most likely never have to engage in combat herself, which came across as an insult. The Marine Corps defines Rules of Engagement as the 'directives that delineate the circumstances and limitations under which United States forces will initiate and/or continue combat engagement'.[12] We listened to the snarky attorney for twenty minutes lecture us on how and when we were allowed to engage enemy combatants and what punishments and/or criminal imprisonments we would face if we broke those rules. One rule I will never forget, which the attorney stated emphatically, was that if we were engaged in a gunfight with enemy combatants that were positively identified and actively shooting at us, and they dropped their weapons and ran, we could, under certain circumstances, be held on murder charges if we continued to engage and kill them. I was shocked and immediately demoralized. I doubt anyone in the room felt differently, except the tone-deaf JAG attorney. We were up against an enemy that would gladly seize the opportunity to capture and brutally torture us to death on video and broadcast that video around the world for our families to see, but we, the good guys, could go to prison on murder charges if we killed that same enemy as they disengaged from a fight with us, only to reengage later. Hard to believe.

Rules of Engagement are necessary. There are many heinous outcomes that can and have resulted from too loosely governed combat units engaged regularly in battle, but still. This brief left me with the sickening feeling that I should be very afraid out there, on the other side of the world, of my own US Government Military Court System and all the possible punitive outcomes I may face should I even by accident slip up in combat. In that moment, it was more

---

12. United States Marine Corps, 'Law Of War/Introduction to Rules of Engagement' (article).

concerning to me than the thought of being maimed or killed on the battlefield that my same government sent me into in the first place. It felt like betrayal. I understood the reasons behind the rules, but it didn't shake the feeling.

We walked out of the briefing tent and were handed our ammo. I pondered all I had just heard as I loaded three hundred rounds one by one into my personal magazines; each individual 5.56x45mm green tip bullet having the same potential of sending me to military prison as the last. I might as well have had one hand tied behind my back for the rest of the deployment. We all felt that way.

MISSION TASKING

While most of us were in and out of briefs, Company and Battalion Command were under way mission tasking the whole Battalion in coordination with Regimental Command. We made our way back to the hooch, where our command staff was waiting to give us the word. Lt (Lieutenant) Huff, our Platoon Commander of Alpha Company 2nd Platoon, huddled 2nd away from the others and let it out: Alpha Company was tasked Sangin exclusively, and 2nd Platoon would be fully operational as a gun-truck Quick Reaction Force (QRF) attached to Marine Corps 2nd Reconnaissance Battalion in the northern Sangin Valley, who was also there in support of 3/5's main effort further south. When we weren't needed on QRF, we would be running our own combat patrols. I couldn't believe my ears. All our hard work in training was actually going to pay off. We 2nd Platoon landed the hottest mission of the entire Battalion and we were ECSTATIC!

There was one caveat, and it was that we would be down one squad. There was another mission that required a squad-sized element in Delaram, and we sectioned off 3rd Squad to man it. They were tasked with what we called a 'Jump Mission', which was a personal security detail for Regimental Command of RCT2

(Regimental Combat Team-2). It would involve a lot of moment's notice VIP travel all over southern Afghanistan. 1st and 2nd Squads, though, were heading into Sangin's firestorm. The other three Alpha Company Platoons would be taking over base security for the three major FOBs (Forward Operating Bases) in Sangin. 1st Platoon was to man security at FOB Nolay, 3rd Platoon would take FOB Inkerman, and 4th would be at FOB Jackson, which would be the location of Alpha Company Command.

I remember wondering what to tell my family. I hadn't spoken with them since I left the States, and they were waiting to hear what mission I had been tasked with. They knew we were most likely going to Sangin, and they knew to some extent how bad it was leading up to our arrival. I was now one of only twenty-six Marines tasked with the highest-risk mission of my entire Battalion in the most hostile combat zone in the Afghanistan war. Everything was about to take off.

Our platoon's attitude stiffened up once again. We began mentally preparing and got laser focused on Sangin's dynamics. The 3/25 QRF unit that we were going to replace was there waiting for us to arrive. The rainy season was just about over but in the preceding 2 months, Sangin had seen a heavy amount of rain, creating swampy conditions on the roads, and 3/25 had not been on patrol as much as they had in late 2010, meaning we were likely to face a fresh barrage of enemy activity. We rehearsed our SOPs (Standard Operating Procedures) for mounted and dismounted patrols and began to assign roles that had not yet been designated. One of those roles was point man, who inherently bears the highest risk on foot patrols. The point man is often the first to get gunned down in the opening bursts of an ambush, the first to get tagged by sniper fire, the first to step on pressure plates and the first to get cut off from the rest of the patrol in a fight if the enemy force is strong enough. There was initially talk about a couple other Marines running point for 2nd Squad and they naturally had some reservations. Sgt (Sergeant) Mathes and Sgt Ashley ragged on them about how long it might be before they'd get their legs blown off, be it on the very first foot patrol or sometime within the first week of operations. It was all lighthearted but unnerving still.

The placement of Marines in patrols is dictated by the specific mission roles they're assigned as well as the weapons they're responsible for deploying. The patrol leader is near the rear, so he has the best vantage point of the battlefield and his personnel. The SAW (Squad Automatic Weapon, belt-fed machine gun) gunner is intertwined in the patrol and his A-gunner is one man away from him helping with ammo reloads, barrel changes, or to take over the SAW if the main gunner is killed. The same goes for heavy machine gunner and his A-gunner. The grenadier is intertwined as are snipers if we have them, and the radio operator is as well. The point man is out front. He is the way finder and navigates the planned patrol route, hits designated checkpoints, is the first to expose himself from cover and concealment and is responsible to lead the way through the IED-infested terrain for those behind him to follow. He is the first to traverse fresh unchecked ground, exposing himself to the highest risk of getting blown up.

While some of the guys bantered with the others, I really contemplated volunteering myself into the role. One of my favorite Bible verses is in the book of John where Jesus said, 'Greater love has no man than this, than he lay down his life for his friends' (Jn 15:13). I saw point man as opportunity to follow Jesus' example of selflessness. I would be taking the risk on myself and alleviating others from having to, at least up to the point I get taken out. I approached Sgt (Sergeant) Peck, my squad leader at the time, and Lt (Lieutenant) Huff and requested to run point. They happily approved and the deal was sealed. What would my parents think? My last trip home I went to breakfast with my dad and a Korean War Veteran friend of his, who emphatically told me through the emotional turmoil of his own wartime experiences, 'Don't you ever volunteer yourself into harm's way. The guys that do don't come home.' My dad was sitting right there when the comment was made. I resolved to just not tell them. Ultimately one of us was going to have to run point. I was nervous but filled with moxie and thrilled to step into the challenging role. Taking initiative is a major emphasis all throughout Marine Corps training. If you see something that needs to be done, you don't wait for someone else to take care of it. You own the issue yourself, take the initiative and make things happen. Volunteering for point man was a small thing relative to the whole but it was an enormously important decision for me and one I felt extremely proud of making.

We were only at Leatherneck for a short period before loading all our gear up and heading to Sangin. A couple of hours ahead of our departure, a few of us went to the closest chow hall, which was a small tent not far from where we were staged. The food was warm, which out there meant it was worth waking up early for. On our way out of the chow hall Sgt Baudin stole the chow hall Marines' big auxiliary speaker. We all started laughing hysterically and ragged on him about it. His stated justification was, 'Meh, they're at Leatherneck. They can get another one.' He wasn't wrong, and it was hilarious.

Our time for departure rolled around and we geared up, said goodbye to 3rd Squad and loaded onto Marine Corps Super Stallion helicopters, which flew us to FOB Nolay on the southern end of Sangin. Nolay sat high on a ridgeline and overlooked the vast green agricultural Sangin Valley. Just an hour or two after we touched down the first explosion rang out in the distance. Sgt Ashley and I ventured over to the base perimeter to locate it and gazed down at a huge grey smoke plume a few hundred meters into the valley. A Marine in a nearby perimeter security post motioned over for us to keep our heads down. We were already being cautious but their motion to us indicated that there actually could be a real-time sniper threat, which surprised me. It wasn't that I shouldn't have already known that, just that even after all the training and preparation, the reality of battlefield risks aren't easy to program your mind around until you experience them. I watched the perimeter security Marine for a few minutes after and noticed how carefully he positioned himself within his post to not be exposed to obvious avenues of fire. It was a good lesson learned early and I'm grateful he was looking out for us.

The entire day, explosions and gun fire rang out in the distance and all day we found high points on the FOB to carefully look out over the valley and try to locate them. Some of the explosions had been controlled detonations, meaning Marine foot patrols found an IED and destroyed it in place with C4. The C4 concussions were distinctively faster than those of the ammonium nitrate that IEDs were comprised of, and it didn't take long for us to be able to differentiate between the two from only the sound and feel of the explosion. In the first two days at Nolay, we witnessed a multitude of explosions, listened to and watched several firefights, watched strafing runs by A-10 Warthogs and witnessed medevac (medical evacuation) chopper pickups accompanied by attack helo strikes; all in just two days and all close enough to Nolay for us to see and hear, which did not account for the many other battlefield happenings that were too far north in the valley for us to witness. It felt like the Wild West, and whether naïve, stupid, or insane, I was so excited. Most of us were. We were finally going to do real Marine things.

OUTSIDE THE WIRE

Our RIP (Relief in Place, also referred to as TOA – Transfer of Authority) with 3/25 began almost immediately. When a new unit takes control from another, leaders from the new unit operate alongside the existing unit for a few days. Then, the units flip, and the new unit assumes operational authority while leaders from the existing unit operate alongside the new unit in an advisory role for a few more days. This overlapping handoff passes the baton of responsibility in a way that enables intentionally real-time information sharing from the existing unit, so the new unit doesn't start operations from scratch. We spent a considerable amount of time with them asking questions and hearing their stories and experiences from the last seven months. We discussed all the enemy tactics they encountered, their experiences with enemy ambushes, counter-ambush assault methods they deployed, firefight distances, RPG (enemy shoulder-fired Rocket Propelled Grenade) attack considerations, IED strikes, friendly and hostile areas, and so much more. On day two, Lt Huff, Sgt Ashley, Sgt Peck, and I set out on our first truck-mounted patrol outside the wire with 3/25 around midmorning from Nolay. There were four gun trucks total, with one of us in each truck.

Early in the war, standard Humvees were the Marine Corps' vehicle of choice. The iconic vehicle was tough, agile and well proven but what we learned from both Iraq and Afghanistan is that Humvees, even up-armored, do not bode well against vehicle-targeted IEDs. In fact, it didn't take an enormous IED to completely obliterate a Humvee and all the Marines inside it. Ahead of our deployment, the Marine Corps adopted two new massive, armored vehicle lines that would become our war horses in Afghanistan. The vehicles were essentially designed around a stout metal hull with a heavily armored underbelly that was strong enough to stay intact during most explosions. This would better shield Marines inside from as much of the explosion's concussion and shrapnel as possible, which was a huge improvement from the Humvees.

The first truck line was the MRAP Cougar, which stands for Mine Resistant Ambush Protected. The biggest and baddest of them was the six-wheel-drive version, which we referred to as the 6x6. It was an enormous, tank-like bus, suitable to operate as a small infantry troop carrier, mobile assault vehicle and more. The MRAP also came in a 4x4 configuration, which was not that much smaller than the 6x6. The 4x4 was what we had most of and we referred to them as just MRAPs. The other truck line was the M-ATV, which stands for MRAP All-Terrain vehicle. Yes, that is an acronym within an acronym. The M-ATV came as a 4x4 and was a little smaller, quicker and nimbler than the MRAP Cougar while still being heavily armored. 3/25 had several of each type of truck, which would all be turned over to us.

When the four of us from 2nd Platoon loaded up to patrol with 3/25, I rode in one of the 4x4 MRAPs and asked every question

I could. 3/25 had not been on the road for the previous week+ given the amount of rain and they were the main gun trucks that patrolled Route 611, meaning it had been more open to enemy activity for a long time. We departed Nolay on the 611 heading north, which ran along the mountainous east side of the valley all the way to Kajaki. The northern region of Route 611 was to be our primary area of operational focus for the months ahead given it had the highest volume of enemy activity. We made our way through the Sangin Bazaar, which sits north of Nolay, and then into the northern countryside. The road was littered with massive holes like it had been intentionally carpet bombed in some places. Every hole was the result of a previous IED explosion, or a recently enemy-dug hole for a new one, and they were everywhere. In some areas only small stretches of road could be driven in a straight line without having to swerve around huge 3ft-deep holes in the ground. These craters often created choke points, which the Taliban would exploit and plant new IEDs in.

The 3/25 Marines seemed like they had details on every stretch of the road as we drove along. 'This compound is hostile to us and sympathetic to the Taliban … This one was owned by a storekeeper who was murdered a few weeks ago by the foreign insurgents for giving us information … The Taliban use that tree to hang flagging markers to the locals when pressure plates have been planted nearby … That alley is often an enemy fighting position for snipers who take shots at the turret gunners when we drive by …' and on and on as we crept along at a 10mph average pace. I was amazed and remember wondering how these guys were so calm about it all when death appeared to lurk around literally every corner. They were just used to it, and that felt crazy.

As we drove further north, we passed FOB Inkerman, PB (Patrol Base) Transformers, PB Alcatraz and about seven clicks (1 click = 1,000 meters) away from our planned turnaround location, we pulled up on another Marine unit that had been hit by an IED and ambushed less than an hour prior. Their 6x6 MRAPs was flipped over and laid out on its side 20m off the road. It looked like a beached whale. All four Marines inside had just been airlifted out in critical condition before we arrived. We were told the IED was a 120lb command pull, meaning there was a trigger man on the other end of a pull string off to the side of the road in one of the adjacent building complexes. The accompanying ambush was light enough that the unit was able to combat it back and once the medevac helo and partnering helo gunship arrived, the enemy shooters went dormant. These Marines were hit less than an hour before we pulled up. Had they not been there before us that morning it would have been us.

We turned around there instead of pushing further north like we had planned. After some time while we headed back south, we rolled up on a freshly dug hole in the road that wasn't there before and it had a distinctive 'ant trail', which is a small trench trailing off the side of the road from the hole to conceal a wire that would be connected to a newly emplaced IED. The enemy was setting up on us. Had we continued up the 611 seven more clicks like we intended before turning around we may have very well given the enemy enough time to finish planting their IED and then two units would have been hit that morning. My truck stopped before crossing over the hole so we could investigate it. The 3/25 Marine in the front passenger seat looked back at me with a smirk and said, 'Ready to get your hands dirty? Let's go check it out.' The driver chuckled. I took a deep breath and said, 'Let's do it,' then went to open the back hatch of the MRAP. I stepped out on the first metal grate stair step and scanned my surroundings. With no noticeable immediate threat, I started to step down to the road and all of a sudden, BRRRRRRRAAAT! An AK-47 auto burst blasted off and rounds whisped and crackled in, narrowly missing the turret gunner.

I jumped back into the hull of the MRAP, slammed the door shut, and the driver yelled 'HOLD ON!' and punched the gas in reverse to get us off the 'X'. The turret gunner was just days away from going home and nearly had his head shot off on one of his very last patrols. Unable to identify exactly where the firing was coming from, we cautiously drove around the hole and pushed south out of the target area to give the enemy the impression that we were not interested in a fight that morning. The 3/25 guys had a plan though. Our driving away would likely draw the enemy combatants back out on the road to try to complete their IED emplacement so we could catch them in the act. As we departed south, an ISR overwatch drone headed to our location. ISR stands for Intelligence, Surveillance and Reconnaissance, which was a fancy label for our aerial unmanned drones, many of which were Predator drones carrying Hellfire missiles. These were our eyes in the sky, and we referred to them as angels of death. The enemy could not see them, but the drones saw everything and when needed they rained down death from above. The drone began circling the IED dig location and locked onto two assailants as they went from nearby building to building. Once we were out of their eyeshot, they went back to the road and started to complete their IED plant just as 3/25 expected. While the drone stayed fixed on the enemy, we pushed a little over a click south (1 click = 1,000 meters) and began our cat and mouse game. After the combatants and one additional counterpart finished their IED emplacement, another unit was called in to approach the target area from the north as an 'unsuspecting' decoy to get the enemy to position themselves to detonate the IED. A 2nd Recon unit responded and began heading that way. As the 2nd Recon unit approached the area the ISR pilot confirmed that the enemy combatants took notice and were setting in for their attack. The decoy unit halted, and the air strike was green lit. A jet patrolling at high altitude in the area received the mission and dropped a 500lb GBU (Guided Bomb Unit) right on top of the small building the three enemy combatants were positioned in, sending a huge explosion and smoke cloud into the air that we watched from a high point on the road less than a mile away. The explosion sent echoes up and down the valley, a phenomenon that I was already becoming accustomed to.

Surprisingly, two of the three combatants managed to crawl away from the explosion and tried to flee the scene, becoming what we called 'squirters'.

The drone finished them off with its two on-board Hellfire missiles. The decoy unit drove up to their location, dismounted and confirmed three enemy KIA. An EOD team (Explosive Ordnance Disposal) then came, and control-detonated the ammonium nitrate that they planted. It was a 100lb command detonation IED, only 20lb shy of the one that had just flipped a 6x6 MRAP, the biggest truck in our fleet, 20m off the road and put four Marines in critical condition earlier that morning. That would have been plenty to do damage to us in the 4x4 MRAPs or MATVs we were patrolling in. As we started back toward Nolay I felt a strong sense of shock and accomplishment. The 3/25 Marines weren't impressed, however. This was just another day on the job for them in Sangin.

This was my first time outside the wire only days in country. We encountered the aftermath of an unfortunately successful enemy IED strike and accompanying ambush, four critically wounded Marines, another IED near miss and control detonation in place, a very close enemy small arms attack, a 500lb GBU drop on an enemy compound and two Hellfire missile strikes from a Predator drone resulting in three enemy KIA: all of this in a matter of just a few hours on my very first patrol outside the wire and it wasn't even fighting season in Sangin yet. When we got back, I took my gear off and told the guys in my squad all that happened. We went into long detailed deliberations about the events along with all the information the 3/25 Marines had instructed us on while outside the wire. The day went on and with it explosion after explosion, gun fight exchanges and air drops all throughout the valley in our distant view, just like the day previous. It really was the Wild West.

READY TO KILL

Sangin was chaotic, but also very beautiful. Outside the urban centers, the region was a massive agricultural valley basin that stretched roughly 2 miles wide and 30 miles long. There were large and small mud building complexes obscurely checkered all over in mixed densities amidst large green fields, thick green tree lines, deep blue water canals and dammed trenches. Dirt roads and walk paths connected it all in an asymmetric fashion and the mighty Helmand River ran down its central/western half. Desert mountains entrapped the valley on the east, west and north. From an aerial view the valley was an oasis in the middle of an arid, tan desert.

The beauty was all misleading, of course. Most of the lush green crop fields were opium-filled poppy plants and the entirety of the agricultural valley basin, which we referred to as the 'green zone', was enemy controlled. Every friendly unit we interacted with told us to be extremely cautious of the green zone and to expect enemy contact every time we stepped foot in it, without exception. It was enemy territory all the way up to Kajaki and they had it completely laced like a trap-infested labyrinth with enemy snares, IEDs, ready attack positions and planned ambush locations everywhere. There were carved out 'murder holes' in the building walls all throughout where enemy fighters could shoot from fortified positions with good escape routes. There were large dead spots (areas hidden from view) everywhere that made for easily concealable enemy movements in volume. While agricultural in nature, the terrain was flooded with deep canals, ditches, trenches and built-up walking paths and roads, many of which were fully concealed by accompanying thick vegetation, which made for excellent covered and concealed fighting positions everywhere. The enemy could easily ambush us and then ditch their fighting positions and disappear when we countered before we could close in on them. Further amplifying the enemy's home field advantage was the fact that the local nationals were interlaced all throughout, meaning the enemy fighters could quickly and easily blend in and pretend to be civilians themselves without anything to suggest otherwise. It was a very complex battlespace for so many reasons.

Reports came down concerning the number of foreign fighters that were in the valley at that time and there was said to soon be a massive influx as spring set in. Before 3/25 left we got word that there was a reputable enemy sniper from Iraq that had just arrived alongside other snipers from Uzbekistan. There were also reports of a new supply of heavy weapons including PKMs, which are equivalent to our M240G 7.62x51mm heavy machine guns and even DShKs (very heavy machine gun) that fire larger rounds than our 50 cal, which are big enough to cut an adult male in half from a single round impact. The environment was very spicy and with the turn of winter to spring it was expected to get much worse.

Patrol number two with 3/25 came the day after the first. By the time we left the wire we had already heard explosions in the valley. We counted thirteen the day prior and that was only those in hearing range from where we were at Nolay. This second patrol was less eventful than the first. We patrolled to Inkerman to link up with another 3/25 squad who also hadn't been out for the past week given the weather. There was a good amount of noise in the valley on our way there, but we made it without any issues. We met the new squad, and they shared their stories and experiences, which were similar enough to the others. We departed Inkerman and pushed north for a while before heading back south to Nolay. Just like the day before, the 3/25 Marines shared all the pertinent information they had. For this patrol the four of us from 2nd Platoon switched trucks to get a wider array of input from 3/25. The new guys I rode with noted how the Taliban would mark IED locations by standing big rocks up on their side rather than their bellies, stacking rocks in piles, carving out bark in trees, or painting seemingly indiscriminate spray paint marks in walls to mark ambush locations, which was all affirming of what we'd been taught during the work-up. The enemy's IED markings were subtle and easily overlooked, but detectable if you knew what you were searching for. The Marines informed me of the locations of several paid secret informants along the 611, one of whom being the shopkeeper who had recently been murdered by the enemy after they found him out. Another one of the informants would hang a certain cloth on a specific corner of his complex wall, which we could see from the road, if he had information to share. These guys were said to be trustworthy enough, but we all had doubts. In Sangin the locals appeared to be looking out for number one only, and loyalty was always questionable.

One of 3/25's running jokes was the IED 'butt pucker' effect. This occurred while driving when you realized you're passing over a patch of road that looks like it could be an IED but by the time your eyes catch it, it's too late to avoid and your adrenaline boost tenses your body up, which clinches your butt cheeks together as you anticipate an explosion right underneath you. We all had a good laugh about it, particularly because I kept puckering up while we were on the road, and they kept calling me out for it. To my new eyes, EVERY variance in the dirt road looked like a disturbed earth patch.

We made it back to Nolay and intermingled with the rest of our 2nd Platoon guys up on one of the outer edges of the FOB. While we conversed, a gun battle sounded off several hundred meters in front of us in the valley and a short period of time later an A-10 Warthog appeared in the distance and began strafing runs. We all paused and watched with a sense of awe. SHHHRRRWWWFFFPHHHH … BRRRRRRRRRAAAAT!!! The A-10 sounded off and littered the ground in its path with a hailstorm of 30mm cannon rounds ripping up everything they touched. Two consecutive runs and then all went quiet. Whoever they were gunning for was dead or too scared to continue fighting. I would have been too with an A-10 targeting me.

The A-10 Thunderbolt 'Warthog' is an air-to-ground jet that was apparently considered for decommissioning in the early 2000s given it was falling behind the times technologically. When the GWOT (Global War on Terror) went into full effect though, the A-10 quickly became indispensable to ground units for close air support. The A-10 has very distinct sounds both from its jet engines and from its 30mm front-mounted Gatling gun. Anyone would be terrified to be its target. Often enough, air support only had to show up for flyovers and their show of force alone changed the dynamics of a ground battle. The A-10 flew off after its strafing runs and the firefight in the distance that preceded it ended.

A few minutes went by as the conversations continued and I noticed a MAM (Military-Aged Male) suspiciously appear from around the corner of a small group of dirt buildings that resided high on a hillside behind Nolay. I quickly racked a round in the chamber of my FN M16A4 assault rifle, planted the buttstock in my shoulder and put my ACOG chevron (rifle scope crosshairs) on his center mass as my heart rate began to rise. My mind raced searching for intent. I thought it would be foolish of him to try to fire on us from that close to the FOB given he was in a position with limited retreat options. Any presentation of a weapon and show of force was all it would take, and I would drop him right there. I had him dead to rights. A few more seconds went by and what initially seemed like suspicious activity showed to be non-threatening as the man went about his business. I let my rifle down and continued watching him while my angst dissipated. I began to think, 'This is the first man I've placed in my crosshairs and had he shown himself to be a credible threat I would have shot him without hardly thinking twice. I would have really killed that man.' It struck me in that moment that despite any reservations otherwise, I was ready. I was ready to kill that man and any others that threatened me or the Marines with me.

Throughout my time in the Corps the thought of really taking another person's life was something that I had been a bit nervous about fully embracing. I just wasn't sure what I might be like after becoming a killer. From the day I joined, I obviously was willing to do it and knew someday I would likely have to, but I had yet to actually face the reality of it. This experience sealed the deal though. I had made the mental shift and broken through a major personal moral barrier. I was ready to kill. I walked over to the trucks and sat down for a minute to say a little prayer. I was not overly emotional, just engaged with the significance of the moment and what it meant to me. 'Lord, carry my heart and protect my mind through all this. Help me to navigate it all honorably, and please Father God, don't let me lose myself.'

Chapter 4

WE'RE OPERATIONAL

'Be polite, be professional, but have a plan to kill everybody you meet.'

General James 'Mad Dog' Mattis

It was early March, and we were fully operational. We completed our condensed RIP with 3/25 and began around the clock truck-mounted patrols from Nolay to the far northern reaches of Route 611. Our mission was twofold in support of the main strategic effort in Sangin. The first focus was to own and dominate the 611 from Nolay to several clicks south of the Kajaki dam and disrupt/disable enemy efforts to emplace IEDs or establish footholds along the route for ambushes on friendly force convoys. Route Clearance Combat Engineer convoys were commonly targeted. They were often tasked to clear additional routes into the green zone, demolish specified buildings, compounds, and walls, and repair the 611 roadways from previous IED explosion damage, etc. They were softer targets than the other fighting-focused units in the valley and got hit a lot. Other supportive convoys were as well. Our second mission focus, which at any given time would subvert the first, was to be an around the clock gun-truck Quick Reaction Force for the region, with the northern valley in primary focus. We were to be the immediate cavalry response to any call for help up and down Route 611. After deliberation with regional command, we were assigned the callsign 'Mesquite QRF', as tether to our unit's Texas origin (the Mesquite tree is a thorney drought tolerant tree found across the State of Texas and is commonly associated with it). We were there to fight for America, but we were Texan Marines and that meant a lot to us.

All-hands preparations went into effect immediately. 3/25 relinquished ten trucks to us with enough weapons and munitions to fend off just about anything the Taliban could throw our way. Grenades, LAW rockets (shoulder fired Light Anti-armor Weapon), AT4s (Anti-Tank rockets), flares, M240G heavy machine guns, Mk19 auto grenade launchers, two of the big, bad 'Ma-Deuce' M2 Browning 50 caliber machine guns and an enormous amount of miscellaneous boxed and belt-fed munitions to feed through all of it. We even had a Claymore or two, which required regimental level approval to use. We were loaded to the teeth. We gave every weapon a hard cleaning, as we did the trucks. Air filters, oil changes, batteries, tune-ups, electronics, radios, and on and on. Just about everything 3/25 gave us was due for TLC (tender love and care) and we breathed new life into all of it. Meanwhile, Lt Huff and SSgt Smith were making introductions and beginning coordination with all the other units in the region.

Once everything was set, we started mounted patrols around the clock. Of our ten trucks, we had four 4x4 MRAPs, two 6x6 MRAPs, and four MATVs. We also had four mine rollers, which were long, extended platforms comprised of a row of closely spaced wheels and tires weighed down by top-mounted metal plates that were designed to run over and set off any pressure plate IEDs ahead of the actual truck tires. They would connect to the front of any truck and be steered by the typical driving operation of that truck. They were not difficult to drive with on straight and flat runs but in the mountainous terrain we were in they certainly added driving challenges. Having them in operation proved to be well worth the hassle though when we started hitting IEDs.

We had only enough Marines to man eight trucks at any given time and we instituted twelve-hour shifts between our two squads to have at least four trucks on the road at all times. We split the trucks evenly between the squads: one 6x6, two 4x4s and two MATVs per squad. 2nd Squad was first up to bat, and we set out in the evening on an all-night security patrol. This was probably my fifth time outside the wire including our patrols during the 3/25 RIP (Relief in Place), but it was our first time on our own and was thus momentous. With hyped up music blaring from auxiliary speakers we set up in our trucks, we traversed down Nolay's steep rocky dirt road driveway at sunset and hit the road north. We acted like we owned every area we entered. Our trucks were the biggest things on the road, and we issued no doubt that we wouldn't smash through anything that attempted to stop us. In the back of my mind were all the videos I had seen of insurgents slipping IEDs under unsuspecting Humvees in Iraq while they were caught up in traffic. We learned that lesson from those before us and made it known that we didn't deviate for anyone. They deviated for us.

We made it into the Bazaar, which was the safest strip of road in the entire region given its density of local civilians. The enemy wouldn't risk high collateral damage in that area given how angry it would make the locals. The Bazaar was also the only stretch of road with solid pavement in Sangin, obviously creating additional challenges to digging-in IEDs. Afghan National Army (ANA) and Afghan National Police (ANP) were everywhere in the Bazaar and while our enemy was also there hidden among the population, they still wouldn't risk hitting us there. They watched though, studying us quietly and intently from a distance just like we studied them. They took pictures of our trucks, pictures of our faces, studied our weapons, studied our gear, and looked for any weaknesses to exploit. We knew they would do that so we postured ourselves extra rigid, always exuding strength and a tone of malice, blasting metalcore songs like *Let the Bodies Hit the Floor* by Drowning Pool as loud as our speakers would allow so that everyone knew not to test us.

We gave the impression that we were ready at any moment to slug it out to the death, and we absolutely were.

Long strip center-like buildings lined either side of the road and most were open faced. Trash was everywhere. Everything was dirty and there was a constant sour burnt stench in the air. To this day I remember that smell and anytime I catch a whiff of something similar it takes me right back. This was the most advanced area of the region regarding infrastructure, and it was rudimentary at best, showcasing how much we had to be thankful for as Americans who grew up in a completely different environment. There were signs of improvement all throughout though. Evidence of our COIN mission's local improvement projects was apparent, and I like to think that there was a hum of excitement for modernization around it all.

We made it through the Bazaar, exiting the township-proper, and hit the dirt road again as we entered the rural region where most of the fighting took place. The further north (or west) anyone went away from the main Sangin urban district, the more hostile everything became. There were only two Patrol Bases in the far north that housed 2nd Recon's Alpha and Bravo Companies, which are much smaller than standard infantry Companies, but both were in the hills to the east. The dynamics up there were notably different than down south, where there were three major FOBs, several smaller Patrol Bases, and outposts that 3/5 units were constantly sending their foot patrols in and out from. Up north, there was no heavy friendly presence and the enemy had deeper roots and a wider sprawl. The 611 was less kept and more difficult to traverse with more choke points and narrows. The people were also more sympathetic to the Taliban and foreign insurgency. It was all around more dangerous.

The music was now turned off and we began to home in as the day's light faded into night. Just before dark gunfire rang out in the distance, and we listened to radio chatter from a friendly unit in a small enemy engagement. Minutes later it was dark, and we were the only thing lit as far as the eye could see. The valley was very dark at night. Of all the homes and compounds that were occupied at night, few of them had any exterior lighting and there were obviously no roadside lights. Our headlights were visible from way far off, making us an easy target, but we had great night vision gear and were armed and ready to squelch any attack that might come. A few hours went by as we patrolled north, stopping at numerous locations to scan certain areas and check suspicious spots along the road. At times we would stop and spread out along a high point for several minutes, turn all the lights off and just watch night-time activity through IR (infrared) screens, NVGs (Night Vision Goggles) and IR binoculars. Given the lack of area lighting at night throughout the valley, it wasn't normal to see a lot of activity outside of people's enclosed compounds, so when we did see activity we locked onto it. It was not unusual to catch individuals high on heroin walking around erratically in the pitch-black darkness or capture someone privately defecating where they thought no one could see them. Much more eerie were the times we would catch someone trying to spy on us inconspicuously, sometimes from very close. In those instances, I would orient my turret gunner toward the suspect and watch carefully for any sight of weaponry or act of aggression. We owned the night but that didn't mean someone wouldn't muster up the courage to attempt an attack on us at some point. Direct action was less likely of course, but IEDs were another story.

We continued patrolling north through the night and eventually reached our planned turnaround coordinate. Each truck carefully reoriented south while the others provided cover, and then we continued patrolling back south. Another hour passed as we crept along at 5 to 10mph watching, scanning, stopping, and studying our surroundings. We were at hour eight into our twelve-hour shift as we moved cautiously across ground that we had just traversed hours earlier heading north. Without any warning or preceding indication, BOOOOM!!! Ashley's MRAP, our lead truck, took our first IED strike. The shock wave shook the 6x6 I was driving 40m behind Ashley's truck and small debris showered down on us moments after the blast. Ashley came over the radio quickly, 'All Vics, all Vics, this is Vic-1. We just hit an IED, but our mine roller took the blast. We're alright.' Relieved, we all fanned out while Ashley's truck quickly moved off the X and we began scanning for a follow-on ambush. Sgt Mathes was in the front passenger seat of my 6x6 manning the radio while LCpl (Lance Corporal) Apgar was in the turret on the 50-cal machine gun watching for anyone positioning to attack us. I was in the driver seat with my IR screen dropped down scanning for heat signatures to orient Apgar toward. Minutes went by ... nothing. Ashley's mine roller was destroyed, and there was no way for us to drive it out. We called in a wrecker crew to come get it and stood fast for two hours waiting for them to show up. Heat signatures appeared on and off the screens but with no clear distinction of civilian or foe. We held steady waiting for an attack but progressively became more skeptical of the likelihood that anyone would try. The wrecker crew eventually radioed that they were minutes out and Ashley got out and walked the area around his mine roller with a metal detector to ensure it was clear of pressure plates. When the wreckers arrived, we amped up overwatch while they quickly rigged up what was left of the mangled metal frame and then we all pushed back to Nolay. We updated 1st Squad via radio on the way, who geared up to replace us on the road. Just around sunrise we drove up the steep, narrow entry road to Nolay, taxied through the ECP (Entry Choke Point) and entry gate and chunked up the duce to 1st Squad, who exited the wire right after we came in.

We cleared our weapons, fueled up our trucks, prepped our gear for our next patrol and then turned in for a little sleep just as the sun became bright over the horizon. Within a couple hours in the middle of the morning, Nolay's CP (Command Post) radioed over, 'Mesquite QRF 1st Squad just hit an IED.' Unreal. It had only been a few hours since ours. Thankfully, the explosion only clipped the lead truck's mine roller, damaging it badly but not completely destroying it, which enabled them to clear the kill zone quickly. That's two strikes in less than twelve hours. After some time waiting to combat the possible follow-on ambush, 1st Squad investigated the blast site and uncovered a command detonation wire, meaning someone was on the other end of the wire pushing the ignition switch to the bomb. The turret gunner in the lead truck took enough debris to the face to draw blood and he was really shaken up by the blast. When we found that out, things started to feel personal.

2nd Squad geared up on standby and waited for 1st to make it back to Nolay. LT (Lieutenant Huff) made his way over to Nolay's CP to catch the daily intel updates as we prepped to head back out, ahead of our twelve-hour shift schedule at that. Once 1st Squad made it back, we took their other mine roller given we were down to only one and we pushed out. We now had two back-to-back, near-miss IED strikes and hadn't made it to day three on our own yet. The next couple of days of patrols were remotely docile for us but not for the valley. The same distinct level of activity resumed with numerous air drops throughout the day, firefights sounding off in the green zone, and IED strike smoke plumes clearing the treetops in eyeshot. The foliage was starting to thicken with lush green vegetation in full bloom. In only one week there was a dramatic difference as if our arrival triggered the start of spring and subsequently fighting season. Things continued to escalate thereafter.

RISING PRESSURES

On March 17, 2nd Squad began a patrol at midnight. At 0600 we made a long stop to stretch outside of FOB Inkerman and then loaded back up and headed north again just as the sun was coming up. In many prior briefs, we were told to pay close attention to the 'changing atmosphere' in local patterns of life as an indicator of enemy activity. That morning was a complete overhaul. What seemed like ALL the local civilians were loaded up in cars and motorcycles with bags of their belongings and they were all heading south. Vehicles were back to back on the opposite side of the road on and off for miles. They were steering clear of us and going well out of their way to be as far away from our trucks as they could when we drove by. Of those not traveling south, kids were not waving and asking for candy like normal, their mothers were rushing them away when we approached, and no one would look us in the eyes. Everyone appeared to be scared. There was obviously something big planned for the day and they all knew about it. There were hundreds of Afghan flags strung everywhere up and down the road and almost everyone was wearing the color brown. Intel had reported that in the vicinity of the many IED blasts in the recent weeks they had identified several MAMs (Military-Aged Males) wearing brown fatigues intertwined with the locals. It seemed that the Taliban told the locals to leave town and they also masked themselves by having all the civilians wear the same color. Reality set in, 'we are headed into a big fight today, no question, and we are the very first unit going north this morning with no idea when the next convoy will be coming behind us.' This was exactly what we had been waiting for – a chance to confront our enemy directly. No more night-time IED sneak attacks. We wanted force on force engagement and we were about to get it. Our alertness grew by the minute. As we traversed north, fewer and fewer locals were in the green zone and along the road until they eventually disappeared altogether. It was us, the road, and an unusually high number of MAMs off in the far distances in every direction watching us while we watched them. There were fake IEDs and indicators all over the place. The enemy had pre-staged stuff all along the road to try to throw us off. 'What scale of ambush are they doing all of this set up for?' I thought it had to be huge.

As we crept along, we got every weapon in my truck Condition-1 (safety on, magazine inserted with a round in the chamber – essentially ready to fire), and Mathes and I rehearsed every pertinent radio channel and callsign. Apgar prepared additional ammo cans up in his turret for quick reloads of the mounted 50 cal. I checked the two grenades dangling in their pouches on my chest rig, put my hand on my TOPS fixed-blade knife that was tucked under my left armpit, tightened all my gear straps, prepped a couple mags for quick draws, and started getting amped up for the fight. This was it. I quietly recited Psalm 27:1–3 to myself as we drove and prayed 'Father God, be with me and my brothers today.'

We made our way farther and farther from other support units into increasingly more hostile territory. We drove up on small group of older men, presumably local elders, who appeared to be discussing the events of the morning. We stopped to try to talk with them and our interpreter, 'M', who was normally very bold, was hesitant to get out of the truck to talk to them for fear that one of them might quick draw and kill him right there roadside. We tried to talk to them anyway, but they wouldn't interact with us, which was a bad sign. The further we got the more everything felt like a ghost town, but MAMs continued to lurk. They peeked around corners, darted here and there on motorcycles in the distance, crouched on rooftops eying us, and stayed positioned for quick cover, like they weren't sure who was going to take the first shots and kick off the firefight. Our interpreter began picking up ICOM chatter as we crept along. ICOM stands for 'Inter Communication', which referred to the enemy's radio communications. They commonly used unencrypted walkie talkies that we would tune our interpreter's green gear radio to and so he could listen to what they were saying and report up to us.

M listened in as they noted our convoy's location, number of trucks, etc. and discussed how they were going to hit us. 'Any minute now,' I thought. I was aggressively scanning alleyways, rooftops, windows, doorways, building corners, murder holes in the building walls, tree lines and fields. 'Any minute now.' We continued to creep along further and further north. Everything remained very still and quiet. 'Any minute now.'

We managed to get to our planned northernmost point for the patrol without a single shot fired. Coincidentally, it was the furthest north we had ever been. We waited anxiously. We stopped and fanned out in a

360° security to wait for them to strike. We all knew the ambush was imminent and we positioned ourselves in strength for the kickoff. We waited. M started picking up ICOM chatter again and it looked like they were getting ready to start the attack with RPGs (shoulder fired Rocket Propelled Grenades). We stood ready. I had my rifle across my lap with one hand on it and the other on the steering wheel. Extra grenades and two LAW rockets were all in arm's reach behind me, along with two fire extinguishers in case our truck took an RPG and caught on fire. We watched and waited. I was more alert than I have ever been in my entire life. This was it. Finally, our moment to face the fire and put the summation of four years of United States Marine Corps warfighting training to the test in the most kinetic battlespace of the war. 'Any moment now, any moment ... any damn moment.'

LT (Huff) comes over the radio unexpectedly, 'Alright, all Vics, all Vics, we're turning around and Oscar Mike (On the Move) back south.' What!? I couldn't believe what I just heard. 'Did he really just say that?' I looked over at Mathes in shock, 'Did he just say that? He can't be serious. It's all just about to kick off!' Moments later Ashley comes over the radio, 'Vic-1, turning around.' I gasped. He really did just say that. I said to Mathes, 'Ask LT to hold for just a few more minutes.' He refrained. I began pleading with LT in my mind, 'JUST 5 MORE MINUTES. THEY WILL HIT US AND WE CAN FINALLY LET LOOSE ON THEM!' Ashley's truck turned around and repositioned south. Truck-2 followed, and then moments later, with great reluctance, I did also ... 'Vic-3 turning around,' Mathes asserted over the radio. One by one each of us turned around while the others provided cover. With each truck making the turnaround, I thought, 'They'll hit us now. We are vulnerable with some trucks facing one direction and now some the other.' Nothing manifested. Every truck made the turn and oriented south. With the turret gunners re-established differentiated sectors of fire, we spread out the convoy and slowly but surely, we pushed south. I was so disappointed.

Within minutes, the Recon COC (Command Operations Center) came over the radio noting a 2nd Recon Squad had declared a TIC

(Troops in Contact) a few miles south of us in a HEAVY gun battle on foot. We were immediately called in for QRF support, so we picked up our pace to get to their position as fast as we could. This was redemption, we were back in queue. We arrived along the 611 adjacent to their location less than twenty minutes after getting the call but they were a few hundred meters into the green zone across the deep wadi that lined the road, and we had no vehicle ingress route to get to them. We were also too thinly manned to send in any dismounts on foot. We set up in 'support by fire' positions in our gun trucks on the 611 in the event the battle shifted in our direction. We also effectively cut off enemy reinforcement ingress from the east, which protected at least one of the ground unit's flanks.

Shortly after we got set, another Recon squad appeared out of the foliage on foot coming down the hillside to our east. They crossed the road between our trucks, each of them stacked with magazines, extra ammo drums for the SAWs, extra ammo belts of 7.62x51mm for the M240G heavy machine gun that their biggest Marine was donning, and several LAW rockets strapped across their backs. They inserted into the green zone calm and collected and headed toward the fight. We sat staged in our trucks on the road two football fields away from the heaviest volume of gunfire I had ever heard for an hour, watching all the exchanges from a distance and eventually ordnance drops and a Huey helo making strafing runs. The battlefield was just barely too far away for us to engage in given the surrounding terrain and it never made its way closer. This was not redemption. This was an insult to injury. We sat on the sideline for over an hour watching the enormous battle from a distance just waiting for our chance to engage, and it never came.

The total battle lasted for maybe two hours and once things settled down Recon let us know they were good for us to push on. It was near the end of our patrol cycle and we RTB'd (Returned to Base) to Nolay. I don't know if I have ever experienced a higher build-up followed by a sharper let down than this. It is difficult to put into words how deflating the whole thing was and why. It was an extremely stressful day for the wrong reasons, one seared in my memory with remembrance of intense negative emotion, and it is a good showcase of the peculiar emotional stress that war can have on a person. I was deeply disappointed about missing out on the fight after so eagerly expecting it. I was also somewhat embarrassed for getting so worked up and being so excitedly hopeful to throw myself into the engagement in the first place. The whole episode was emotionally taxing and highlighted the importance of being disciplined to stay calm and collected.

We all made it back inside the Patrol Base in one piece, no gunshot wounds, no severed limbs, no one killed, in our unit anyway. Given circumstances that preceded this particular patrol, 2nd Squad had pushed roughly thirty-one hours without sleep and the multiple adrenaline rushes had taken their toll. We pulled into the Nolay entrance and past 1st Squad, who exited the wire right after we entered. We refueled our trucks, prepped our gear to head right back out, and then tried to get some sleep. The afternoon was spent resting as much as we could. 1st Squad made it several hours into their patrol and took another IED strike. This one seemed to be bigger than their last one, giving off a much more powerful concussion. No major injuries again, but we lost our third mine roller. 2nd Squad was called up to their support, losing yet another full sleep cycle. We pushed out not long after receiving the call and after locating and escorting them back to Nolay, we rolled right into our next patrol.

After the third IED strike, the decision was made that we would no longer be driving with our headlights on at night. We would now be fully blacked out. Our trucks were equipped with 10in infrared screens that flipped down like a visor in front of the driver. The screen depicted the terrain well enough, and it was great for monitoring night-time activity while stationary but utilizing it for night driving was another story entirely. It felt like focusing intently on a laptop that someone else was holding as a means of seeing the rough mountain road well enough to drive on. My brain just couldn't track well with the unusual and mismatched movement. The result at times was extreme nausea for hours while I drove at night, often accompanied by pounding headaches afterward. It was awful. The only other option was the use of personal NVGs, which was equally miserable, for hours on end. Despite the challenges, we were a massive target at night with our headlights on and this was the right approach after already receiving three IED strikes in such a short period of time. Once that decision was made, I found my way out of the driver seat and into the turret for patrols every chance I got.

Nightfall came as 2nd Squad made our way up and down Route 611 for the next few hours on pace with a typical security patrol, stopping to check out any IED suspicions, which were very frequent, or just to sit and observe. We never stayed still in vulnerable locations for very long though. Late into the night we began pushing far north, deeper and deeper into what infamously became known as 'Indian Country'. The further we rolled through the pitch-black night the stiller things became. I was caught in a heavy struggle to stay awake while maneuvering through the narrow passes avoiding potholes from previous IEDs, sheer drop offs down into the wadi that lined the west side of the road and compound walls that ran alongside the east. At one point I looked over at Mathes, noticing he had succumbed to his struggle and was knocked out completely. I regularly reached back and tapped Apgar's leg to make sure he was awake. Our turret gunner was our first and main line of defense if we got attacked, not to mention his vulnerability being immediately exposed to gunfire and shrapnel. He had to always be alert.

The radios had been unusually silent for twenty minutes-plus. We were all really gassed after so many days with so little sleep. As we crept along in our typical convoy spacing 40 to 60m apart from truck to truck, the road began to veer left enough that I could no longer see Truck-1 from my Truck-3 position. Truck-2 continued around the turn and BOOOOOOM!!! An ENORMOUS explosion blindsided us, sending a huge concussion through the convoy before we even realized what happened. I watched in total surprise as the dirt plume grew higher and higher. Truck-2 was completely engulfed in a dust and smoke tower that stretched higher than I could see the top of through my windshield. I grabbed Apgar's leg and yelled out 'GET DOWN!' as if I had to say anything at all. Seconds later, metal parts of Truck-2 and other debris showered down on us, slamming into my hood, windshield, and the truck hull like debris thrown down from a tornado. Apgar popped back up after it settled and quickly scanned for ambushers.

We immediately fanned out, established our sectors of fire, and braced. NVG's up, IR cameras scanning, waiting for the first burst of enemy fire. The IED appeared to have been a direct hit. The MATVs couldn't take IED blasts as well as the MRAPs and, even worse, our convoy was now split, hindering our ability to repel an attack. Mathes immediately started trying to raise comms with Truck-2. Garcia, Peck and Ramirez were in it and not a word was coming back to us. 'Vic-2, Vic-2 this is Vic-3 how copy over … Vic-2 this is Vic-3 how copy?' … Complete silence. 'Vic-2, Vic-2 how copy? You guys okay?' Silence. From my vantage point, as the dust settled, I could roughly make out the shape of Truck-2, but it was mangled and without any flicker of taillights, cab lights, etc. Concern grew by the second … 'They're freaking dead. Is it all of them or only one or two? Which ones? Do we need to rush in for aide? Will we step on pressure plates if we do?' It was all remarkably tantalizing.

The first sixty seconds following the blast crawled by and our anxiety grew. Mathes decided to go survey the carnage. Just as he started to open his door the radio sounded off. It came through broken, but we could make out what was said, 'All Vics, all Vics, be advised this is Vic-2, we are alright, say again we are alright.' Mathes and I looked at each other with a huge sigh of relief. 'Thank you, God. Thank you, thank you, thank you …' Mathes and I both vocalized. 'Apgar, Truck-2 is good!' He let out a big sigh of relief. The explosion initially killed their engine and radio, but they managed to get it back up. We called in for support and, being the closest unit to our position, 2nd Recon's Bravo Company jumped to and headed our way. As we waited for the enemy to engage, M picked up ICOM chatter. There were two triggermen reporting to their higher ups. They were asserting that they had 'just killed a bunch of Americans', and were still in view of our position. They said they would sit tight until we left so that they could plant another IED to get the next convoy. We all let off the tension, no immediately pending ambush.

We were stationary in hostile territory, a long way off from friendly forces in the middle of the night with our enemy staring us down and obviously within our reach but we had no idea where they were or any way to locate them. We could hear everything they said to their counterparts over the radio but could not identify their position. In every direction there were compounds intertwining the ups and downs of the surrounding terrain and they could have been in any one of them. So could a bunch of civilians though. The longer we sat, the angrier I got. Day after day we had been driving up and down the 611 maintaining a presence, disrupting IED emplacements, locating new enemy activity, and standing ready in a moment's notice to rush into any gun battle, but we kept getting hit with sneak attacks by an elusive enemy that we couldn't locate or retaliate against.

Bravo Company showed up within the hour. They brought an EOD (Explosive Ordinance Disposal) team that analyzed the blast site while the rest beefed up our perimeter security so we could determine if Garcia's truck was drivable enough to get out of the area. As far north as we were and at the time of night that it was, we were not going to get any wrecker's help and we couldn't wait there all night or the enemy would for sure organize a measured attack against us. We decided to give it a college try, and sure enough Garcia's truck hobbled along very slowly on the three good wheels and tires it still had. Bravo Company escorted us and after some time we made it to their meager patrol base in the desert hills east of the 611. Once inside the wire, we circled up and assessed the damage. It was a very, very near-direct hit. The blast went off just behind the driver near the rear tire, blowing the left back end of the truck nearly clean off and obliterating the wheel and tire.

I walked over to Garcia and hugged him. This one was too close. Cpl (Corporal) Garcia and I started in the Marine Corps together four years prior in the same boot camp training platoon. Now we were on the other side of the world together and he was one of my best friends. Immediately following our embrace, I squared up with him and somberly said, 'Bro ... the Monsters [energy drinks] were in the back of your truck.' His face turned gaunt. He hadn't realized that yet. Call it dark humor but that was a pressing thought I had after the blast. The first was, 'Dear God, they're all dead,' quickly followed by, '... and the Monsters were also in the back of that freaking truck ...' ha ha. Garcia managed to get his hands on a full case of Monster Energy Drinks at Camp Leatherneck when he escorted M there via helicopter ride a week prior. From then until now Garcia and I had vigorously traded watches over the case between the two of us, given that any of the other Marines would gladly jump on the chance to steal one or two cans if we weren't looking and there was no telling when or if we'd ever be able to replenish the supply. Our latest stash placement was an empty white ice chest that we kept caged in the open air back of Garcia's MATV. As I followed his crippled truck down the road to Bravo Company's Patrol Base, I was able to get close enough to see that the ice chest had somehow made it through the blast, but I was sure the concussion must have ruptured all the Monster cans inside. We somberly made our way to the back of his truck, looked at each other, and then at the cooler and opened it fully prepared to see the worst. In one of the greatest turnarounds of the week, less than half of the cans had ruptured, and the rest were fully intact, some bloated, but salvageable. Laughter and jumping excitement broke out between us and we reached in and cracked one open, cheers'd to being alive, and sipped down the most refreshing hot, sugary, carbonless syrup that we'd ever tasted. This was one of the best highlights of the entire deployment. Garcia skirted death and some of the Monsters made it out with him.

Bravo Company offered to escort us down to Nolay. We pulled the blown wheel and tire off and did our best to install the spare. Half of the lug bolts were seared off in the explosion, but we managed to get the spare wheel and tire on tight enough to at least give it a shot. Sometime after 0200 (am) we geared back up and pushed out. It was slow rolling, but we were moving. I followed Garcia's busted truck all the way south, waiting for the new wheel to break off and pummel a building along the road, but it never did. We made it all the way to Nolay in one piece and just in time for sunrise.

Garcia's hit made it four IED strikes on our small unit. We were now down two mine rollers, one truck, and a third mine roller was on the brink of being completely unusable. This last strike was very close to being a direct hit and we were obviously rolling the dice on how much longer we would make it before one really smashed us in the face. We were also burning the candle at both ends, repeatedly going twenty-four to thirty-six hours with practically no sleep, often only capturing a couple hours here or there leaning over in a truck seat to break those periods. We all got strung out real fast. Something had to change. A couple of days after Garcia's brush with death, the change came, but it wasn't at all what any of us expected.

MISSION REFOCUS

Arriving at Nolay, we dropped our gear and Garcia and I took his busted truck to the junk yard, which was filled with other explosion-destroyed combat vehicles and equipment. Some of them were charred black from having been consumed in fire, others were riddled with bullet and shrapnel impacts, some splattered with dried blood stains and all of them heaped in piles of destroyed parts. It was a sight to see. We parked his truck among its new crippled companions and stripped it of all weapons, munitions, and other useful gear. With one final look, we contributed our MATV offering at the scrap metal altar and went to pick up a replacement truck from the Regimental Combat Team 2 Motor Transportation unit.

Given the non-stop pace we had been pushing, LT got us off all patrol rotations for the day. We spent the time resupplying, washing clothes and taking showers for the first time since arriving. Up to that point, I had been wearing the same pair of cammies every day and would switch out my boxers and socks every five or six days. Dirt was so embedded under my skin that it wouldn't scrub out and while used to it, we smelled awful. While the rest of us resupplied, LT met with regional commands and negotiated a new mission focus for us. Our current operational method was not sustainable. We were being hit left and right and were pushing crazy hours with extreme sleep deprivation.

When Huff returned, he had an extra pep in his step. Something was up and it was good. He energetically huddled up both squads and let it out, 'Gents, our request for a new mission method was granted. We'll spend the rest of the day packing up, inventorying supplies, and replenishing anything we don't have an excess of. Each of you will skinny down your personal gear to one pack and we'll be leaving the rest locked up in a room adjacent to 1st Platoon's muster area here on Nolay. All of you should make a call home today. We've been assigned our own AO (Area of Operation) and tonight, we're moving up to our new home at Patrol Base Alcatraz. It's about to get even more real, and you should all be thankful.' No way! My jaw must have been on the floor. This was so unexpected but exactly what we needed. PB Alcatraz housed elements of 2nd Recon's Command and their own Alpha Company. It was as remote as things got in Sangin, right in the heart of enemy territory in the northern valley. Our newly assigned AO was north of PB Alcatraz and was the worst stretch of road on the 611 for IED strikes and ambushes. 3/5 owned the south, 2nd Recon's focus was on the inner green zone north of FOB Inkerman and PB Fires (among other places), and our focus would be Route 611 north of Alcatraz and the eastern green zone that accompanied it. We were still to be the on-call QRF gun trucks for the broader stretch of Route 611 north of Sangin's urban Bazar, but while not specifically tasked elsewhere we would be running our own missions in our new AO.

Our plan was to surveil the 611 and eastern green zone through a static picket line of trucks up in the hills along the east side of the valley while running combat foot patrols into the green zone to make contact with and kill the enemy and to disrupt their IED activity along the 611. This was just what we hoped for, a chance to finally brawl with our elusive enemy up close. Every inch of the green zone was enemy territory, and they would attack any unit that stepped foot in it. That had been the governing rule even before the Marine Corps took the region from the Brits. This was as real as it gets, as if it weren't enough so already. 'Hunter/killer foot patrols and ambushes on the enemy day and night in the green zone,' LT said in his briefing. We were now finally tasked with a mission on the offensive that was sure to drum up enemy altercations. Were we ready to go head to head with the enemy? In many ways absolutely. In others, we were about to find out. This was the high-stakes mission of aggression we wanted though. We were finally going to get our chance to go slug it out.

By this point, most of the guys had written their 'final letters' to their loved ones should they be killed. Marines from other squads were designated to be the bearers of those letters in case several of us in the same squad were killed at the same time. I tried on more than one occasion to write my own 'If you're reading this ...,' letter and I just couldn't put the words together. Writing a letter like that validated the real possibility of being killed and then the mind games begin. That letter would also be the last words communicated to my family and would thus be so weighted and defining of me. I just couldn't do it and I quit trying.

I reluctantly decided to call home before we left Nolay. Mom was at work when she answered. She was ecstatic and filled with joy. We small-talked, laughed and enjoyed hearing each other's voices. Before we ended the call she told me, 'Son, have a good attitude, be humble and don't be a complainer. Don't entertain complainers either.' Her words really impacted me while in the incredibly stressful environment I was in, and I still carry her advice today. I called Dad right after, who happened to be in the middle of writing me an email. He and mom both asked plenty of questions and I shrouded my answers while basking everything I did say with heightened positivity. They had no idea what I had already been involved in or what I was heading into, and I certainly wasn't going to tell them. In the back of my mind I thought, 'This actually could be the last time they hear their son's voice. End it on a high note.' I kept a positive bent throughout both conversations, assuring them that I was right where I was supposed to be, that God had his hand on me, and that I was completely at peace with all my decisions that led up to this moment. Before I got off the phone with each of them, I told them how much I loved them, that I missed them dearly and that I was so proud to be their son.

I walked out of the call center with a pit in my stomach. 'What if that really was the last time? What else should I have said to them? Did I honor them enough?' I was a little emotionally frayed. I went to check my email before heading back to my truck. By the time I logged in my dad had finished the email he was in the middle of writing me. At the end of his message, he said the following: 'Stay focused on what really matters and pay attention to detail. When the time comes, dish it out with no reservations and all the fury you can muster. Give them hell son. – Dad.' A wave of emotion hit me in that moment and a weight fell off my shoulders. A father's words can be so powerful, and his approval was second to none. I was eager to be in the fight and was at that point completely resolved to pull the trigger without hesitation when the time came, but deep down I still felt a heaviness from it all. Reading those words from my dad shot right to the issue as if he was speaking directly to my inner man saying, 'It's okay son. I understand and approve of what you have to do.' I wrote Dad's words on my Kevlar as a reminder every time I geared up that my father approved of the often rage-fueled harm that I was tasked with inflicting on other human beings. Right or wrong, in that moment I needed his validation, and I had it.

> 'War is cruelty. There is no use trying to reform it. The crueler it is, the sooner it will be over.'
> William Sherman

Chapter 5

MURDER HOLES AND KILLING FIELDS

'Keep alert and stand firm in the faith. Be courageous, be strong.'

1 Corinthians 16:13

It had been another long period of no sustained sleep as our departure from Nolay was delayed due to other operational happenstances, but we finally made the move to PB Alcatraz and set up camp. Alcatraz consisted of three large mud structures high on a hill east of the 611. Two comprised of only four walls with no overhead cover and the third was Observation Post DeYoung, a monstrous medieval castle-looking dirt fortress that sat proudly pronounced along the edge of the 611 overlooking the valley. It was the outer muscle of the PB with excellent visibility of every avenue of approach and had an unbeatable 180° reach into the valley, making it the perfect machine gun and sniper nest, mortar observation post, etc. It was located on the southern tip of PB Alcatraz. Word was that for years the Patrol Base position had been a major Taliban stronghold, but the Recon Marines took it by force in the preceding months. Apparently, on one of the first days that Recon had it under their control, one of their own, Sgt DeYoung, was killed by an IED as they were clearing the area, prompting the honorary naming of the OP. Alcatraz had no Hesco barriers, concrete barriers, fences, or any continuous perimeter of any kind except for the dirt walls. All that separated the PB from the valley was a couple of perimeter gun trucks with a string of concertina wire along the ridge in front of them. It was a very rudimentarily fortified patrol base, but filled with Marines you don't want to tussle with and I guess that was fortification enough.

We occupied an inside corner of the larger four-wall compound on the northern side of the PB. Our set-up consisted of cots lined along the inside face of the thick dirt wall separating us from the green zone with our trucks at our feet and one camouflage net posted up in the corner that would serve as a place to congregate, keep shade on our already sunbaked food and water supply and set up maps for mission planning and briefs. The huge PB burn pit was literally right beside us and it burned and smoldered on and off twenty-four hours a day. I could just about throw a wadded-up piece of paper into it from laying down my cot. Some of the guys' cots were no more than 15ft away from it.

Burn pits were on most (if not all) of the military installations in Afghanistan and some of them were enormous. At Alcatraz the burn pit was a simple, vehicle-sized dug-out hole in the ground that we threw everything burnable into each day and night. We kept it burning around the clock with diesel fuel. When I say we threw everything burnable in it, I mean everything. MRE trash, water bottles, our own human waste, broken gear, all plastics, cloths, rubbers, thin metals, chemicals, and on and on. If the wind was not specifically blowing away from us, the smoldering black toxic smoke engulfed us, which was sometimes for hours without relief. The only way to completely escape the toxic haze was to be out on patrol. These burn pits are said to be the 'agent orange' of OEF. There have already been plenty of veterans die from diseases onset by toxic exposures from burn pits at the writing of this book, and there will be many more after. We all knew how terribly bad it was for us, but we didn't have a choice. More importantly at the time, the most immediate life or death threats were right outside the walls, not within them.

After setting up camp, we began preparing for our next mission. 1st Squad was getting ready to head out to set up their forty-eight-hour observation picket line and 2nd Squad was preparing for our first foot patrol into the green zone the next morning. Reflecting on that moment just before I went to sleep that night, I spent time journaling:

'I just finished cleaning my weapon and prepping my gear. Of all the days so far in this deployment I think tomorrow may win the title "The Defining Day". 1st Squad is about to depart Alcatraz to set up the picket line in our new AO. They'll be parked +/- four hundred meters from truck to truck. They will live in their trucks for two days straight independently located in separate positions but hopefully in full view of one another if the terrain allows it. If any of them come under attack they will be on their own until we can reinforce them. My squad will head out on our first foot patrol into the green zone early tomorrow morning to search selected compounds suspected of being used by enemy forces. We just had a sniper from 2nd Recon come over to brief us on his experience in the green zone. He reiterated a certainty of making enemy contact and insisted we increase our ammunition load outs in the event we get pinned down for any lengthened period. He admonished us to maintain an aggressive posture and exude strength at all times because the enemy fighters are more emboldened to hit harder on weaker-looking units that they think they can decimate. He said emphatically, "Boys you're heading into the killing fields. Act like a bunch of fucking dick-swinging bulls and they'll fear you." He said the two grids we are going into are among the worst with the heaviest attacks and a high density of pressure plates. He asserted, "Don't play the Taliban's pressure plate game. When you make contact, pin them down and drop ordnance on their heads. Don't be quick to pursue them. That is what they expect and are planning for." We motioned in agreement. In closing he said, "Good luck boys, stay vigilant and kill 'em all." We shook hands and he walked off.

'On the verge of what seems like certain battle, I spent today in prayer. I really don't fear for myself. I am sure I will be nervous tomorrow but for now it is a stretch to say that I'm even concerned. God holds my future. Even should the worst occur, God brings some of the most amazing outcomes from the worst situations and in the span of eternity the tragedies we suffer in this life will eventually not matter much at all in the way they do now. Should tomorrow be my final day I am at peace with my eternal destination, and I thank God for that. I am concerned for my brothers though. I ask the Lord every day to protect them, to send angels concerning them, to show them who He is and draw them to himself that they would have the same eternal assurance that I do.

'We are finally sleeping under the stars again tonight. They are as vast and bright here as they are in the Texas Hill Country. I am reminded of a scene from *Forrest Gump* as he describes a beautiful starry night that partitioned days of chaos in Vietnam. I think also of a quip from a Korean War documentary I watched a couple years ago where a Marine Colonel explains a barrage of artillery fire from both sides in the middle of the night followed by the most magnificent display of stars and a quiet peace on the battlefield that followed. That is what I feel, a sensational quiet peace under this starry night ahead of what may be the biggest test of my life.'

INTO THE BREACH

> *'The Lord is my light and my salvation, whom shall I fear? The Lord is the stronghold of my life, of whom shall I be afraid? When evil men advance against me, and my enemies attack, my heart will not fear. Though war break out against me, even then I will be confident.'*
> Psalm 27:1–3 (abbreviated)

Our mission was to patrol on foot inside grid Q5X in the green zone. Our plan was to insert at the 605N (northing), search and assess the areas around buildings 61–63, 70–73, 56 and 9 for IED materials, weapons, explosives, and any other evidence of enemy activity. At 1315 (pm) we departed from PB Alcatraz. At 1400 we dismounted from our trucks, foot patrolled 400m south on the 611, traversed across the wadi system and dropped into the green zone to begin our search. At 1415 we declared a TIC, Troops in Contact.

My gear was fastened tighter than normal. I had twelve mags on me loaded to full capacity. My rifle was well cleaned and lubed. I had two grenades strapped to my chest, my TOPS fixed-blade fighting knife under my left arm, four tourniquets in different, grabbable locations across my torso, three smoke grenades, two flares, an extra SAW drum, a metal detector, and plenty of water in my day pack, alongside my plate carrier and other typical gear. We loaded into two MRAPs and departed PB Alcatraz in full expectation of a fight. As we drove, I quietly recited Psalm 27:1–3 and asked God for strength. The trucks stopped at the 605N. I opened the back hatch of the MRAP and dismounted. This was our first foot patrol in enemy territory, and I was first out as point man. I made my way 400m south on the 611 with the rest of 2nd Squad behind me patrolling in Ranger File formation. My rifle was at the ready and I surveyed the road closely for disturbed earth, command wires trailing off into the green zone, and other IED indicators. My head was on a swivel going from the ground, to buildings, to rooftops, to tree lines, and back to the Marines behind me. My attitude and posture were brazened. My jaw was clinched, my chest puffed out and my face as scowled as I could make it. There were two voices in my head. The first was that Recon sniper, 'Act like a bunch of bulls and they'll fear you.' I embodied that. The second was my dad, 'Dish it out with no reservations and all the fury you can muster …' I was ready to scrap. Rifle, grenades, fixed blade, bare hands, or rocks on the ground, I was weaponized and in the zone.

Very quickly the pattern of life shifted. All eyes were on us. The locals watched intently to figure out what we were planning to do. I made it to our insert point into the green zone and started in, making my way down the roadside embankment carefully watching for signs of pressure plates and then into the wadi that lined the eastern edge of the green zone. The wadi was flowing with cold water that came up above my waistline. For a nostalgic moment I was reminded of being back at the San Marcos River in the Texas Hill Country where me and my friends would wade through the cool clear stream without a care to speak of. This was quite the opposite though. I was on the other side of the world with 100lbs of combat gear strapped to my body wielding weapons and explosives that I fully intended to use, and I was actively hunting men who were hunting me right back.

I crossed to the other side and set up security for the rest of the squad. The locals were scrambling to get out of the green zone. Men and women grasped their children and darted east in volume. It was all setting up just like we had been warned. Team-2 (my team) made it across the wadi and got set, interlaced in a thin tree line and established quick sectors of fire to cover for Team-1. Everywhere in our view were potential enemy fighting positions. All around us were tree lines, compound avenues, door and window openings, murder holes in seemingly every building, rooftops, and more, each presenting their own unique opportunity of being 'the one' that issued the first deadly blow. There were too many to cover. Team-1 began pushing across the first field toward building 61, which was 100m in front of us. They moved slow, carefully surveying the fresh ground they were on as they traversed across a lush green poppy field. Before they made it 20m across, M, who was with us in Team-2, picked up Taliban ICOM chatter and called out, 'They're about to hit us!' This wasn't good. Team-1 was in a wide-open field at our twelve o'clock. Lt Huff radioed to Sgt Ashley that we were about to get hit and then almost immediately BRRRRRATTTT - BRRRRRRRRRRAATTTT!!!!!! The enemy started in on us from multiple positions as the sound of machine gun bursts and incoming rounds enveloped us. Everyone hit the deck. Despite all my training and mental posturing, the moment those rounds raddled off I froze in a brief state of shock, and everything hit slow motion. I remember watching Team-1 drop to the dirt, alongside my counterparts in Team-2 while I sat still, perched up on the wadi berm on one knee like an idiot waiting to catch rounds in my chest. I remember a feeling of subtle disbelief as my mind raced to reconcile the reality of the moment. I had been fully convinced that we would be in a gunfight that morning, but it was still so surprising when it actually happened.

It only took a couple seconds for me to snap out of it and I dove to the ground and began returning fire into the most likely enemy positions while trying to locate where they actually were. Noticing Mathes 15m in front of me in a small run-off stream, I belly crawled as fast as I ever have into it upstream of him and then reassumed firing at movement behind the compounds in front of us. There were small dust clouds from the enemy bullets fired close enough to the dirt walls they took cover behind, and we began focusing our aim accordingly, chasing them from one position to the next and trying to catch them crossing doorways and other openings. Team-1 couldn't have been in a worse position. They were maybe 40m in front of us at our twelve o'clock laying down in an open field and about 60m away from building 61. They were individually semi-concealed in the 2ft-tall thick green crop stocks but were right in the middle of the crossfire, with no real cover or obstruction in front or behind them. Some of us in Team-2 were reluctantly having to fire right over their heads. Buildings 61–63 were connected by a long wall stretching 100m that the enemy shooters were covered behind and they were maneuvering their fire through various murder holes and doorways along the wall, letting out a long burst from one position and then disappearing to another while one of the counterparts let loose from somewhere else. Team-1 engaged, despite their precarious position, and we all fought to beat down the enemy's fire and gain superiority so we could control the battlefield. Mathes yelled '203 OUT!' and lobbed a 203 HE (high-explosive) round at the compound. The grenade clipped the top of the exterior wall and exploded, sending part of the concussion back toward us. Just after the round exploded, an enemy fighter lifted up from an adjacent rooftop to reposition and LCpl (Lance Corporal) Blair in Team-1 let out a SAW burst that dropped him. Mathes loaded another 203 round and sent it. This one landed shorter than the first between Team-1 and the compound and served as our first major warning of how easy friendly fire could be. I looked over at Mathes and saw the shock on his face. It could have been a bad round with a dampened gunpowder reaction, but it still packed an explosive punch when it landed. Mathes reloaded another 203 HE, this time with noticeably heightened caution.

From the moment the firing started, LT gave notice to command and began coordinating air support. Within minutes we had two helo gunships inbound. At this point we seemed to have 'gained the initiative' by establishing battlefield fire superiority and Team-2 held in place while we all maintained a steady pace of alternating suppressive fires and select shots in the various murder holes, trying to catch the combatants as they popped up to fire. Team-1 managed to crawl up against a couple of small berms in the field and, once set, Team-2 also adjusted position down along the smaller branch wadi that I had moved into alongside Mathes. We maintained contact on and off until the gunships showed up. An Apache and a Huey began circling the area and the enemy shooters that were still engaged with us stopped firing and turned for cover. Team-1 scrambled to mark the target compounds with smoke grenades, but they were positioned so close to it without any cover to egress to and there was a high risk of blue-on-blue friendly fire from the air. The helos performed a couple mock strafing runs instead, which gave us a brief window to reposition for our next move. While doing so, word came over the radio that a Recon unit a few clicks south had also just declared a TIC and the helos gave notice that they would depart our position to help them. Under the helos cover though, Team-1 had moved 20m north of their first position into an irrigation ditch along a walk path. They kept their distance from the compound, where pressure plates would have likely resided.

Now it was our turn. LT gave a heads up, 'Longgrear we're about to move, get ready.' All eyes were on me, the point man, first to leave cover and advance across an open field that had just been riddled with gunfire toward a new building. A rapid analysis screamed through my mind, 'We are in a battle lull and both us and the enemy have now regrouped. Our helos left and I am about to get up and move across this open field with no cover straight toward the compound that the enemy most likely repositioned themselves in and I'll be target number one when they open back up on us. If there ever be a time get shot in the face this is it, and I am walking right into it. So, this is what it means to be point man.' LT gave me the word, 'Longgrear push forward.' My heart was pounding, and fear hit me hard. I started quietly reciting Psalm 27 again and a surge of faith welled up in me. I postured myself with strength reminded that I had nothing to fear and pushed straight toward building 70. Walking speedily through the crops across unchecked ground, fully aware of both the risk of stepping on a pressure plate and getting sniped, I continued reciting the prayer King David recorded from his own wartime experiences. 'The Lord is my light and my salvation, whom shall I fear? He is the stronghold of my life, of whom shall I be afraid?' Step after step with my rifle at the ready I scanned the corners, door opening and roofline of building 70 while trusting that my other Marines had me covered everywhere else. I was ready at any moment to re-engage whoever popped out to draw on me. I looked back to scan the rest of the patrol and noticed that most of Team-2 was still in the wadi, except for Sgt Peck, who was 30m behind me. LT appeared to be tied up on the radio with the Command. I looked at Peck, who gave me a nod to keep pushing and I continued another 40m. I was now far ahead of Team-1 and starting to close in on building 70. My heart was racing again as I anticipated the enemy's opening shots. I continued to scan the potential firing positions that I was walking straight towards, raising my rifle at some to peer through my ACOG (Advanced Combat Optical Gunsight or rifle scope) and continued taking step after step.

Without any warning, SSSNAP! A single shot rang out from building 70 right at me. I hit the ground quickly and immediately realized that my entire body was numb. I couldn't feel anything and was completely uncertain if I had just been shot or not. I frantically crawled up to a small path embankment in front of me. It wasn't good cover, but better than nothing. Peck screamed out from a distance, 'LONGGREAR ARE YOU HIT!?' 'LONGGREAR!!!!' I yelled back 'I DON'T KNOW!' and then started to belt out an ADDRAC (Alert, Direction, Description, Range, Assignment, and Control) while trying to catch my breath. I was in a bad position with no good options. After a few seconds, physical sensation started to come back, and I ran my hand up and down my body. I didn't feel any external blood flow or any sharp pains. 'LONGGREAR!! ARE ... YOU ... FUCKING ... HIT ...!!?' I screamed back, 'NO, I'M GOOD, I'M GOOD!' The enemy shooter had the drop on me for sure and I felt the round whisp and snap, but they missed. Thank God they missed.

In the middle of the field with minimal cover and only semi-concealed, I scanned buildings 70–72 through my ACOG hoping to identify the shooter before they steadied their aim and put their next round right between my eyes. It should have been an easy shot for anyone really trying given how close I was and I didn't have any good options to move to. Now that we had confirmed that these buildings were enemy controlled, the building wall extensions in front of me were likely to be laced with pressure plates. There was the wadi but that was now 80m behind. I stayed put and feverishly tried to locate the shooter while waiting for the guys behind me to motion their advance. Seconds went by that felt like minutes, no follow-on shots. Even in the vulnerable position I was in, they did not re-engage. I got a second lease on life at that moment, an opportunity sometimes not afforded to others.

After a short pause while Peck and I stayed put covering for the rest of Team-2 to join us, LT came over the black-gear radio ordering both teams to consolidate along the main wadi. 'What?' I was less than 100m from building 70 and we had barely started the patrol. We still had much more on the patrol plan to accomplish. Peck affirmed the order and in unison he and I got up to move while Team-1 covered us. Unknown to me and Peck, Command ordered us out of the green zone immediately. The Recon unit that received our helos minutes prior were now pinned down in a heavy fight and reinforcements were enroute to their location. Should we take any casualties or get pinned down ourselves, no reinforcements or air support would be readily available to us. So, we began to egress. Peck and I carefully but hastily made our way across the long field to the wadi with our backs now turned to the enemy's position, which was extremely uncomfortable, even with the other Marines covering us. We got set on the other end of the field and covered Team-1 and the rest of Team-2 as they bounded toward us, stopping to also provide cover for others' movements. Once they were near us and positioned for security, I turned and crossed the wadi. As soon as I got up to cross, the enemy opened back up again with automatic fire and rounds started raining in. We returned fire and began bounding hastily across the wadi and over a 3ft-tall wall that resided on the other side. The first few of us made it over and began suppressive fires to cover the rest of the guys trying to get across. We were now back in a heavy exchange with combatants positioned in these same buildings 61–63 and 70–72 while trying to get out of there. Mathes was the last one to make it over the wall and the moment he crested it, an incoming PKM (enemy heavy machine gun) burst put rounds whistling right through our position, some skipping off the top of the wall in arm's reach of Mathes and few feet away from my face. They split right through our squad as we returned fire but did not touch one of us. 'MOTHER FUCKER!!!' Mathes belted out. I kneeled up and started ripping rounds as fast as I could, fanning the enemy shooting positions, until Mathes was over the wall. Several others did the same. Mathes was enraged and his face turned cherry red. He almost took a burst in the back. It was freakishly close for all of us. We continued to return fire and I got up to course our path out to the road for extract from our trucks that were enroute to meet us.

Under fire from what was now behind me, I crouched low as to not catch a round in the back of the head while navigating through a new group of compounds that we found ourselves in. My internal tempo was redlining from alertness and situational engagement. I advanced carefully, scanning the swath of new murder holes, rooftops, and shooting avenues in front of me trying also to keep my eyes to the ground to recognize any pressure plate indicators. My mind raced to analyze it all so I could react to whatever threat presented itself first and my anxiety hit fever pitch from the overwhelming stimulation. There was too much information to process effectively, and the enemy was still shooting at us. Taking step after step with my rifle planted in my shoulder ready to fire on anyone that presented a threat, I froze abruptly, immediately realizing that something was wrong with the ground beneath the foot I just took a step with. I looked down and to my shock my toes were just a couple inches across the crest of a basketball-sized freshly dug and refilled disturbed earth patch. There was a string coming out the side of it wrapped and tied around a fragment of faint green fabric as a flag indicator to the locals so they would not step on it by mistake. I almost just became 1/23's first amputee and it felt like my heart stopped. Just a couple more inches and I would have set off the pressure plate IED right underneath me and checked out of Afghanistan for good. Given how low I was crouched down in avoidance of the incoming rounds behind us, it probably would have blasted my head off and killed me on the spot anyway. I slowly backed off and regained my composure while searching all around me for accompanying IEDs. God forbid the point man lead the squad right into a cluster of pressure plates. Cautiously concluding that it was a sole placement, I called it out to the guys behind me, who passed it along throughout the squad as each Marine came up on the booby trap. We continued to push with extreme awareness and eventually the roadside came in view. There was now a row of compounds and walls between us and the enemy fighters and they eventually backed off their gunfire. We posted up in 360° security until the trucks pulled up minutes later. I stepped out, flagged them down, and we loaded up and headed back to the Patrol Base. Every one of us just went in and made it out of the green zone on foot unscathed, but barely. The green zone held up its reputation and we finally got our small taste of it.

We all had a sense of shock and awe in those trucks, but that was wildly overshadowed by exhilaration. Those of us who'd yet to encounter combat, which is arguably the greatest achievable milestone for any Marine, finally got our chance. For young Marines who had painfully sacrificed so much to be molded into American warfighters, engaging in combat was a rite of passage, a proving ground and one that is held in the highest honor. We finally made it, and we were all thrilled about that.

All of us learned things about ourselves that day. You try your hardest to envision how it will really be while in training but there is no way to grasp how it feels to have the enemy you are endeavoring to kill actually try to kill you back. Our operation overall was not perfect, but no one crippled under the pressure. It wasn't the all-out brawl that it could have been either had we rushed those buildings but that was because we restrained ourselves from playing into the enemy's booby trap tactics. We stood our ground and repelled the attacks that came at us while continuing to advance our patrol until ordered to pull out. For this first engagement on foot, that was good enough for me.

Our enemy had three easy opportunities to land their shots. When they first opened up, Team-1 was 60m from one of the compounds the enemy was firing from, and in the open with no cover. When the single shot was fired at me, I was in the same situation and when the enemy shooters engaged us the third time, half of the squad was still coming across the field to the wadi with their backs turned. Despite this we managed to seemingly take out at least one if not more of them and avoid any hits ourselves. Back home, my grandparents had committed to praying Psalm 91 over me and my unit every single day. 'Because he loves me, says the Lord, I will deliver him. I will protect him because he acknowledges my name.' I thank God for his protection that day. There were plenty of opportunities for things to take a turn for the worst, but they didn't. The patrol and combat engagement were relatively uneventful compared to some, but for us in that moment it was an enormous success and huge confidence boost.

A humorous notable mention: when the firing started and I moved down into the branch wadi, Mathes was half submerged just downstream to my left. During a brief lull in the shooting, I realized the unique opportunity that I had been presented with and I let loose a full bladder, which naturally flowed down stream and engulfed him and all his gear in my floating bubbles. I began to laugh and when he asked why, I told him through laughter and pointed at the white bubbles attaching to him. He looked around himself and back at me in anger, letting off some expletives as I laughed even harder and then the firing kicked up again and recaptured our attention. It was fantastic.

SURVIVE THE NIGHT

Back at Alcatraz the mood was energetic. We tended to our gear, ate MREs and prepped for the next day's patrol. Evening turned into night, and we received a call from LCpl Salines's truck on the picket line. He was having brake issues and needed help. Another truck was having radio problems as well. During the work-up, I had a fair amount of time learning how to diagnose and address issues with the trucks, so Smith and Huff tasked me to run to each truck and fix their issues. We used the opportunity to resupply them also. Me, Garcia, Turner and Gil loaded up in the 6x6 and departed.

We pushed out late in the night dropping off water and batteries to the first two trucks, and then took Turner to the third, which had the radio problems. Turner was impressively engineer-minded and took it upon himself to be our radio expert in the absence of one in 2nd Squad, which proved to be indispensable as problems inevitably continued to occur. After we patched them up, we pushed to the fourth truck that had air brake issues. It was pitch black outside when we arrived. The truck was positioned up on a steep incline east of the 611 in a narrow inlet with obstructions on either side. Salines told me that he lost all pressure in his brakes, meaning if his parking brake gave way it would send the MRAP barreling down the steep incline and crashing into the green zone on the other side of the road.

I had the guys back our 6x6 up the incline right in front of the busted MRAP, close enough that I could hook up our truck's 5ft coiled air lines to the connection points above their front bumper and refill their air system. I hooked everything up and started pumping air. There were two hose connections on each truck and one of the connections on their truck broke its seal and started bleeding air during the refill. I went in between the two trucks to tighten the connection and the moment I touched the line the connection head blew off. The MRAP's brakes immediately gave out and the 32,000lb truck that was perched up on the steep incline took off and smashed into the back of the 6x6, knocking the guys inside the truck out of their seats. Gil screamed out 'LONGGREAR!!!' Last he saw, I was right in the middle of the two combat vehicles. I yelled back, 'I'M ALRIGHT, I'M ALRIGHT.' I couldn't explain how though. I remembered reaching out to adjust the connection when the line popped off and then watching the MRAP smash into our 6x6 from beside both vehicles. I was right in the middle of them when the line broke, fumbling my feet around on the loose rocks beneath me trying to not slip down the incline, and in what felt like an instant I was beside them watching one smash into the other. Another incredibly close call that I narrowly avoided.

At this point the 6x6 was holding both trucks in place on the incline. Given the robust steel structure of both MRAPs, the collision damage was not significant on either of them. I climbed up on Salines's hood, reached down and re-engaged the brake lines and started filling again, this time with added caution. After a few minutes Salines's air pressure gauge showed the system replenished and all looked good when I tested it. I packed up the hoses, made sure the guys in the picket truck were good to go, and then we pushed back to Alcatraz, pulling in just before sunrise at 0530 the following morning.

It had not been twenty-four hours and I flirted with death five times. The first machine gun bursts of the enemy's ambush where I froze in place, the single shot at me while I approached building 70 in the open field, the enemy's re-engagement while we egressed, the pressure plate that I almost stepped on, and now this, almost being crushed to death between two massive combat vehicles in the middle of the night along a mountainous, IED-infested roadside. I pulled my gear off at my dirty, smoked-out cot and thought about the conversations I had with my parents a few days prior. They nearly lost their son numerous times in the past twenty-four hours and obviously had no idea. It was now day three at PB Alcatraz and our next combat foot patrol was hours away. I debriefed with SSgt Smith and others, received an atta boy for completing the night's tasks, and hit the rack just in time for direct sunlight in my face.

Within a couple of hours I was awoken to begin prepping for our next foot patrol. Intel reported that the Taliban had already set up in fighting positions in the grid area we were heading into. The mission was like the day prior's: insert, survey specific compounds for enemy assets and activity, scan fields adjacent to the 611 for command wires and repel ambushes that befall us. We all doubted we would get very far into the mission without resistance. The day before we didn't even make it fully to our first compound before we were locked in firefight.

Another Recon guy came over for us to consult with. He said we were 'nuts crazy' for not going into the green zone with any heavy weapons the day before and asserted that we were very lucky to have come back out without any casualties. He insisted that we should never step into the green zone without at least one M240G (heavy machine gun) per foot element to beat back the PKMs. He said the enemy fighters out there weren't afraid enough of the SAWs (which are considered "light" machine guns because they fired the same smaller sized 5.56mm bullets that our M16/M4's did). If we wanted to ensure superiority, we needed heavier rounds, and plenty of them. Why didn't the sniper tell us that the day prior? LCpl Ramirez prepped a couple of our extra M240Gs for foot patrol carry and we distributed extra ammo belts to be carried by various Marines.

Within thirty minutes of that conversation LT walked back from the CP (Command Post) and said, 'Change of plans boys. 1st Squad is RTB (return to base) right now and we're headed down to Nolay for refuel and resupply.' This came as a surprise and disappointment. We only barely scratched the ich in the previous day's battle. Nobody said it, but I suspect Recon shot down our patrol plan on account of us being too thinly manned without 1st Squad's involvement, and especially after the enemy resistance both us and the other Recon patrol encountered the day prior. We all conceded and reorganized accordingly. 1st Squad made it back and we loaded up into our trucks and started south to Nolay.

KEYS TO THE KINGDOM

Nolay was the southernmost FOB in Sangin, and was closest to Camp Leatherneck, which was the Marine Corps HQ Base in Helmand Province. Nolay also had a very defensible helo pad area and fuel station and it seemed to be the biggest supply hub in the valley. Jackson and Inkerman were smaller FOBs further north and the rest of the establishments in the region were small Patrol Bases where supplies were trucked in or less frequently dropped off by helo. We had to regularly refuel our trucks anyway, so all our food and water came from our own pickups when we were down at Nolay and those trips were at all times of the day and night intermixed with our patrols. Each visit presented an opportunity to raid the chow tents and scrounge around for anything other than MRE food. If we were lucky, we would hit Nolay in the middle of the night when no one was guarding the food supply, enabling us to sneak into the supply shipping containers and nab whatever we wanted. We became more ruthless in our raids as time went on.

On one random occasion, we stopped at Nolay sometime after midnight. While waiting for LT to return from Nolay's COC (Command Control Center), I made my way over to the chow tent to see what I could find. It was as dark of a night as any, and I had the keys to the kingdom it seemed. I quietly slipped into the tent, which I excitedly found to have just been freshly restocked. After filling my pockets with as many cliff bars and beef jerky packets as I could fit, I picked up an entire case of thirty-plus Snapple Iced Tea cans, which was the newest item in stock that had been intentionally placed for distribution during the following morning's chow. Elated, I quietly exited the tent, case in hand, and prepared my escape back to the truck. As I was just about to round the Hesco barrier chow tent entrance a shadow appeared, which sent me into a panic. With no time to react properly, I set the case down behind my feet and leaned up against the Hesco with my arms crossed. I was caught red handed, there was no escaping it, but I tried to play it off nonchalantly anyway. I had no other choice. At the tail end of the shadow was a sizable food service Marine with white apple ear buds in both ears, who was sweeping off the plastic grate walk path that we were both standing on. I looked right at him waiting for his skepticism to kick in and unravel my robbery. He looked up at me and nodded upward in the 'what's up' fashion. I responded in kind as my eyes skewered in bewilderment and he turned his eyes back down to the ground and continued sweeping without skipping a beat, disappearing behind the adjacent Hesco on the other side of the entrance as he swept along. I was white-eyed shocked. How could it not click in his mind how suspiciously out of place it was for some random Corporal to be just chilling by himself up against the entrance to the chow tent in the middle of the night? I picked up the case of Snapples and bolted in the direction he had just come from to get far away before it all hit him, and he came back to confront what he had just been initially oblivious to. I could not believe what had just happened, but it was awesome. I cracked open a

Snapple as soon as I got back to the truck and stashed the rest deep under my gear behind my driver seat so that prying hands would struggle to rip off my freshly stolen booty. I never liked Snapple before, but out there it was better than any tea I had ever tasted in my entire life.

After the previously mentioned canceled patrol, we left Alcatraz and arrived at Nolay around 1200 (pm). We refueled, resupplied, and went to hang out with the 1st Platoon guys. When we pulled up, they were boasting half-gallon Blue Bell ice cream containers, and we were immediately jealous. Huff went to the COC to get the latest intel and came back with plenty of updates. Among all the updates, LT told us there was a new arrival of thirty to forty fresh foreign fighters who had entered the northern valley the preceding day and with them a heavy supply of new gear and weaponry. There were many more to follow. These influxes of foreign troops accelerated in volume and frequency as fighting season was now in full swing. Many of the incoming fighters were combat experienced and posed a much greater threats to us than the untrained locals. I don't know if ironic is the right word, but the fact that those fighters were sent or volunteered themselves into Afghanistan to fight after having trained in another nation for the preceding months, just the same as us, made it all feel like a giant proxy war.

We left Nolay later that day and made it back to Alcatraz in the late afternoon with our new stock of sunbaked, microplastic-filled water bottles, MREs and a new MRE alternative called First Watch. They were packaged like MREs but comprised of different varieties. This was quite the exciting new thing as we were so sick of eating the same MRE options day after day. We unloaded and huddled up to discuss the next day's mission plans. LT raddled off his Five Paragraph Order without a hitch as usual and we took notes, discussed all the various mission dynamics, and began preparing. The plan was for 2nd Squad to provide truck-mounted support for 1st Squad, who would be dropped off at the 611N under the cover of darkness so that they could get positioned to monitor the area during sunrise. They would then patrol south along the 611 searching for IED emplacements, signs of enemy activity, etc. It was 1900 and our departure was to be at 0400 the following morning. I prepped my gear and laid down under the stars on my smoke-stained cot with my black Zondervan study Bible as my pillow. I said a prayer while gazing into the clear night sky and quickly fell asleep.

We woke up at 0230 and geared up for the patrol. Self-gear checks, buddy-gear checks, truck checks, all other checks and we pushed out. We quietly departed Alcatraz at 0400 blacked out, arrived at the 611N around 0440, dropped off 1st Squad and fanned out for mounted fire support. The sun rose and the pattern of life began to shift as quickly as the locals realized 1st Squad was already there on foot. People started making their way out of the green zone, crossing the 611 and congregating in the hills to the east. It was amazing that the locals were inclined to so quickly leave the soon-to-be battlefield when we entered but only to congregate right across the road, which was very much in range of stray rounds, long-shot RPGs and indirect fire. They would sit for hours on the east side of the valley and just watch the battles take place. It always felt strange having an audience, but I guess being unable to tend to their fields while we and the enemy occupied them, they didn't have anything better to do.

While the locals were exiting the green zone there were a number of MAMs entering into it a few hundred meters to our north and south and congregating behind the first line of compounds across the crop fields. My eyes fixated on two in particular. For several minutes, they studied us, talked among themselves, and moved around to view us from different angles. I called them out to my turret gunner, who oriented toward them, and I zoomed in close with my IR screen to see if they were armed. Even though it was obvious who they were, they never showed themselves to be an imminent threat and eventually disappeared behind a compound. 1st Squad began moving down the 611 searching for IEDs. LCpl Finnern had our black labrador retriever, Rosie, up and down the road sniffing for ammonium nitrate. Rosie was far from the picturesque military attack dog, but she was a fantastic bomb dog, not to mention the morale boost that having her around provided us. She had already found several IEDs on the 611 in the previous weeks that we had EOD teams blow in place.

Blair's truck had the GBOS camera extended up in the air and they were scanning the valley from over the treetops. The GBOS was a high-powered camera that could provide clear video while zoomed in over a mile. It was fixated on the back side of the MRAP and could be lifted 30ft in the air, giving us a valuable vantage point from the 611. On this stretch of road, the wadi ran right along the roadside and 1st Squad didn't cross it, keeping their foot patrol in close proximity to the trucks. Tensions rose as the minutes passed. The pattern of life change suggested that an attack was imminent. Everything got very still and other than the locals up on the hillside to the east, no one was in sight. Eventually M started picking up ICOM on his green gear. He said the enemy was trying to coordinate their attack and kick it off with RPGs to the trucks. On hearing this we quickly repositioned them and periodically made sporadic truck movements to throw the enemy off. Our turret gunners scanned likely RPG firing positions to try to catch the triggermen before they could let off their shots. 1st Squad continued patrolling down the road while we waited for the enemy to hit us, but they never did. The foot patrol made it all the way to the planned extraction point at the 603N and loaded up. Several buried command wires were found pre-staged for future IED connections. Their locations were noted and reported up to Command, who dispatched an EOD team to come and dispose of them.

Among all their tricks, the enemy would booby trap their planted IED wires, or lace their trails with pressure plates, as many other patrol elements had learned the hard way already. We maintained efforts strictly to locate them and let the explosives experts deal with the risks. We provided area security as the EOD team came and went and then we made our way back to Alcatraz without a shot fired, which was disappointing to 1st Squad given we 2nd Squad beat them into the first gunfight. The dynamics were there but things never tipped over.

Chapter 6

TANKS OF SANGIN

> *'There are only two kinds of people that understand Marines: Marines and the enemy. Everyone else has a second-hand opinion.'*
>
> General William Thornson

As the days progressed our operational pace and range of mission activities were all over the map. We were on the road at any point throughout the day or night responding to calls for reinforcement, road security, investigation of suspected IEDs or enemy activity, routine check-ins at the three major FOBs and more. Every day the valley was still filled with the echoes of explosions, gun battles and the roar of air support periodically thundering overhead. Everywhere we went we received intel briefs with the latest information and our knowledge of the environment, our enemy, the locals and progress of the broader war effort grew exponentially fast. We were tuned in. We were always in discussion with someone about regional dynamics, operational methods, new enemy tactics, etc., always trying to stay a few steps ahead of the enemy and not succumb to the temptation of developing routines. In war, routine kills. As soon as a predictable pattern is established, the opposing force, whether us or the enemy, exploits it and hits at the most vulnerable point within that pattern. The Taliban hit bigger and harder if they had an advance indication of where we would be or what we would be doing at any given time. We were constantly sharpening our operational methods, both mounted and dismounted. On foot, we worked toward being quicker, lighter and quieter, getting right to where we were going at any given time and doing our thing before the enemy had a chance to set up on us.

Our tactics for actual enemy engagements were almost completely different from our conventional training. The experiences that 3/5 had endured from the enemy's many pressure plate strategies had overhauled our typical gun battle methodology. The strategy that seemed to be most successfully implemented in the valley during that time in the war was to locate, engage and consolidate or entrap the enemy to then drop ordnance on them. This differed from the standard Marine Corps infantry method of closing in on an enemy position and killing them up close through fire and maneuver. Our standard aggressive assault tactic was well known by the enemy, and they regularly used it against Marine units before us by baiting them into assaulting through pre-staged booby-trapped areas. Additionally, given how volatile Sangin was in that time of the war, we all had a substantial amount of air assets in support including various types of helicopter gunships, A-10s, HIMARS rockets, Predator drones and jets. The moment any unit in the valley declared a TIC over the radio, anything available headed to that unit's support almost immediately. Once engaged, if we could just fan out and flank the enemy's escape routes, pressuring them into a consolidation of sorts, we could rain in death from above without having to charge forward and expose ourselves to the pressure plate risks. These tactics were very restrained but a lot safer for us.

Night diggers were on the rise in late March. We spent a considerable amount of time on Route 611 at night already but not often on foot. Night missions came with greater risk given reinforcement support was much more challenging. After several days of consecutive IED strikes in the same vicinity though, we decided to organize a night-time recon mission on foot so we could sneak in and try to catch the enemy in the dark. Command gave us the green light, and we were pumped. Our plan was for 1st Squad to drop off 2nd at the 575N around 2200 and drive off. We would then quietly patrol a few hundred meters south on the 611 and insert into the green zone, cross the first crop field, and set up in two fire team positions along the first tree line roughly 200m west of the 611 in between compounds. This would give us plenty of vantage in that area as well as put us right in the middle of the enemy supply crossway from compound to compound. If we could sneak in effectively, we would be able to catch our enemy in the act and take them out without them knowing what hit them. The trick after the fact would be successfully getting out once we flagged our position but at worst we could hunker down in place and defend ourselves until morning. We were all very confident that even if we did come under a high volume of fire, we still had the upper hand because of our night optics and that we would be the first mover in the fight.

I was extremely excited about this one. It was high risk, high reward and about as high speed as it got for us. When 2000 rolled around we geared up. Extra batteries, extra water, extra grenades, fixed blades, IR optics, radio checks, medical gear checks and other gear inspections. We went through additional self-checks and buddy checks to ensure we had every piece of gear covered and that it was all strapped tight. In addition to my personal NVGs, I had a rifle-mounted night vision scope affixed in front of my ACOG. Should things get really close, we had plenty of grenades and blades. We were charged up and ready. When 2100 came around the wind picked up. Ten minutes later, the air was filled with dust and a storm surge started to hit. Ten minutes after that, Command canned the patrol. It was a huge letdown, but the right call. Getting strung out in enemy territory with no reinforcement support is how units get into trouble. That being said, the IED planters we may have eliminated now had another night to plant their bombs unchecked.

We turned in for the night, whipped out our single-person tents and slept through the storm, which was welcoming because the rain beat down the burn pit smoke while we slept. The next morning, we got up and prepared for another 2nd Squad foot patrol. To break up our patrol 'pattern', we planned three quick inserts and extracts. The first was an insert at the 619N to hit compounds 29 and 23, then extract at 623N; the second was an insert at 630N and extract at 634N, which was a dummy insert just to throw the enemy off; the third was an insert at 637N to hit compounds 33, 31, and 47 and extract at 639N. If it all worked out this was a good opportunity to really confuse the enemy by getting in and out quickly with no real intention of engaging.

We geared up and set out. Reaching our drop point, we dismounted and started our entry into the green zone. I made my way down the roadside embankment through the IED threat zone (dead space between the roadside and adjacent compounds) and as I started to cross the wadi an enemy AK-47 burst shot off near our front truck. It was just a few shots and from only one combatant, which seemed odd. I continued into the green zone with added caution and once I made it across the wadi Command called us up for immediate mobile QRF support of a Route Clearance Combat Engineer convoy that was pinned down under a very heavy attack north of our position on the 611. Those pop shots now made since. They were decoys intended to lure us in and distract our attention so our trucks wouldn't continue north toward the unit under attack.

We quickly ran back to the trucks, mounted up and headed north to the unit in distress. The Combat Engineer unit sustained a big IED strike, disabling one of their MRAPs in place, and they were taking really heavy RPG, RPK (enemy "light" machine gun) and AK machine gun fire. We pulled up in the heat of it with machine guns raddling off in all directions. Our turret gunners quickly joined the party and let loose on the dust clouds coming from the enemy fighting positions 50 to 100m into the green zone. We quickly beat them back into a brief lull, giving us a moment to position our trucks in between the engineers' convoy and the enemy fire. We rapidly set up a cordon security containing them, and they started rigging up their truck to tow it out. In this particular location the first line of compounds to the west were just across a 100m wide-open flat accompanied by a swath of thick green trees. The scene felt like a huge trap. The insurgents didn't ever hit this hard while that close to the road. The closer they were to us, the less likely they'd be able to escape alive. Their ace in the hole had to have been that 100m flat, aside from the IED they had successfully hit the other unit with. I suspect they had it set up as a minefield that they hoped we would aggress through, which explained their apparent boldness in staying engaged so close to us. They even had Taliban flags propped up in the middle of the field to taunt us. They were trying to lure us in. We tried to stay as close to the roadside as possible to avoid hitting any follow-on IEDs and we were hesitant to dismount for the same reason. While the engineers were busy rigging up their busted truck, our turret gunners scanned the west anticipating the next exchange.

All of a sudden, an enemy shooter popped around a corner, taking aim at our lead MATV and fired an RPG before our gunners could get a shot off at him. The explosive projectile screamed through the air in an instant and clipped a small extension wall off a roadside compound that was situated barely enough in the way to catch the round and it exploded, showering everything in the vicinity with shrapnel. It was CLOSE. Just another foot or two over and it would have cleared the wall and been a direct hit to the cab of the MATV. Immediately following the explosion, rounds rained in again. Our front two trucks hammered down with the 50 cal and a M240G. Our rear two with another M240G and the Mk19 auto grenade launcher. LCpl Greer was on the 50 right in the middle of the battlefield and he was laying waste to the enemy shooters while the guys in his truck spotted them, directing him toward other muzzle flashes in view. Greer killed several shooters throughout the exchange.

I was in the rear truck while all of this was going on. I requested permission to dismount and take a team into the green zone at our southernmost point to hit the enemy at their flank, giving us an L-shape ambush on them. I was so confident we could hit them without them realizing where it was coming from, and we were far enough back from the 100m flat that the pressure plate threat didn't seem as severe. I was denied twice. Command already had air support enroute. A jet was on the way with a 500lb GBU (Guided Bomb Unit). Our machine gunners fended off the enemy shooters until eventually the radio transmission came through, 'BREAK, BREAK: ALL UNITS, SPLASH IN 30 SECONDS, SAY AGAIN SPLASH IN 30 SECONDS. ALL UNITS TAKE COVER.' We were danger close for sure to one of the biggest bombs in our arsenal. The turret gunners crouched down in their turrets, and we all braced for impact, hoping the coordinates were on point. Seconds later … SHHWFFBOOOOOOM!!! The GBU hit center in a compound 100m west of our position and put out an enormous concussion that made our ears ring in the trucks. When it dropped, we all went wild. The firing died down and started to fizzle out as the enemy combatants that were still alive bailed. We maintained security for the following hour until the Combat Engineer unit was mobile. They headed back south to Nolay and we returned to PB Alcatraz.

When we got back to PB Alcatraz additional details about the engagement came to light. The MRAP that took the IED blast had the front end blown off from a direct hit. Quickly after the explosion the enemy launched a very aggressive attack. The IED also disabled the Mk19 that was mounted on the targeted 4x4 MRAP. As the Marine in the turret scrambled to get it back up after having just been knocked delirious by the IED explosion, he took two enemy bullets to his torso, dropping him down into the truck hull and wounding him critically. In an act of extreme courage, a female Corpsman who was in the back of that same MRAP opened the escape hatch behind the turret in the ceiling of the truck hull, stood up through it and started ripping rounds at the enemy with her M4 to suppress so another Marine could try to get the Mk19 up. As the life or death situation ensued, the enemy fire shifted to the now exposed female Corpsman. While she actively engaged the enemy, one of the incoming enemy rounds caught her in her left arm, which was propped up holding the foregrip of her rifle as she fired. It hit her just under her left elbow, traveled through her arm and exited out the back of her shoulder, nearly severing her arm off completely. She also dropped back down into the busted truck as the rest of her unit fought to keep the enemy fighters from overrunning them. It was quite an ordeal and, fortunately, we were already outside the wire not far from their position when their call for help went out. I never heard after if our two wounded survived their combat injuries or not.

At this point in the deployment, we began to really come into our own. We were bullish in our operations, confident in our strategic thinking, creative in our tactics and very heavy-handed in the blows we dealt. We had plenty of close calls already, though without any serious casualties, and it was on all our minds how much longer it would be before that changed. Everyone paid the piper in Sangin, and it seemed obvious that we couldn't be the only exception.

Tension began to show between LT and some of the more senior enlisted, which was not unexpected or uncommon. LT wanted to maintain command control, but some felt like he was overbearing. At times he'd brush off advisement from some of the more senior guys who had been on several deployments already. They did the same to him though. The position he was in wasn't an easy one and at times we were not an easy group to command. This was Huff's first deployment but there was not another Platoon Commander in 1/23 better suited for our mission than he was. Lieutenant Huff graduated top of his OCS class. He was a marathon runner built like a UFC fighter with a calm, but commanding demeanor and we respected him. In Sangin, we were isolated from our Battalion and Company, operating somewhat autonomously in close coordination with 2nd Recon in the most kinetic battle space in the war. We had a unique purpose to fulfill in support of the larger comprehensive units in the region. We had limited resources, were thinly manned and were under the highest performance expectations given the daily high-stakes situations we were engaged in, but we were making it happen and eager to do so.

In one of the most bolstering happenings of the war for us, we received word in a regional intel report that the broader Sangin insurgency, both Taliban and foreign fighter cells, had come around to assigning a title to our unit. This was huge. This was enemy recognition and in war that means something. When we got to Sangin, we were regularly told the enemy referred to the Recon guys as the 'Black Diamonds' because of the very visible black diamond shape-NVG mounts on the front of their new-generation Kevlars. To the enemy, the Black Diamonds were to be feared. That's what we wanted. We wanted them to fear us and to be weary and disheartened by our hard-hitting retaliation should they feel emboldened enough to attack us. The day finally came. From ICOM communications, local informants and other regional intel sources it had been confirmed that the enemy officially titled us 'The Tanks' in their internal communications. Their understanding of our little element was that we were the main predator gun trucks up and down Route 611. We were also told that they had communicated to their larger forces to take extra precautions when attempting to hit us and, if possible, to let us pass by and target other units. Hearing this was an enormous accomplishment for us. It validated that we posed a high stature and threat to the enemy.

We received fresh intel of another new influx of foreign fighters that had arrived and some of them were snipers. Our informants provided us descriptions of specific Soviet and Iranian sniper rifles among other things, and the word was that some of these snipers were Uzbek and Chechnyan and were in the valley to be paid per kill. They were there to hunt us. It was unnerving given we were now performing more foot patrols. The first burst of an ambush is the most opportune time to take us out on foot and the greater number of enemy snipers just increased the odds. Among all the strange dynamics of how this war was fought, the way the foreign fighters came and went among the locals never sat right. Almost every day on the road we would pass by cars, vans, motorcycles and even trackers filled with military-aged males mean mugging us fiercely and it was obvious who they were. We just let them drive right on by like nothing was wrong, allowing them to amass behind the scenes and eventually attack us. It was all very frustrating but that that's just how things worked at that time in the war.

SMITH'S CLEAN SHOT

One of our next patrols focused on a long list of possible new IED emplacements that Command wanted us to investigate between the 59N and 62N. With 1st Squad as the foot patrol element, we pushed down to the 59N and started making our way north, utilizing our dogs and metal detectors to try to locate IED paraphernalia at all the specified locations. Thirty minutes into the patrol, M began picking up ICOM chatter. The enemy was discussing our movement and getting ready to fire on us. We relayed the message to 1st Squad, and they quickly fanned out and began closely scanning our surroundings to try to locate the enemy. 2nd Squad did the same in our trucks while we all anxiously listened into M's reports of what the Taliban were communicating. We were about to get hit from any number of possible locations and positioned ourselves to quickly react. As the foot element in the front of the patrol progressed cautiously, Greer took notice of subtle movement through a small door opening less than 30m ahead of him. He quickly set up his M240G on a small stem wall along the roadside and just as he was aiming in to be ready to fire, a single shot rang out from behind him and he watched the figure behind the doorway collapse instantly. It was Smith that fired the shot and had just taken out the enemy shooter that Greer was lining up on. Greer told us later it was a clean 'pink mist' shot to the head that killed the combatant before he hit the ground. After the shot was fired, ICOM transmissions went silent. We continued up the road with much greater precaution, expecting an enemy reprisal, but none came. Throughout the patrol, 1st Squad found command wires trailing off into the green zone and we reported each location to Command, who dispatched a reinforced EOD team to dispose of them. We eventually reached the planned point of departure and 1st Squad loaded up into the trucks to head back to Alcatraz. Another successful patrol.

The next day, we set out to inspect the remaining potential IED emplacements but in a very unconventional fashion. Given the day prior's standard drop off, patrol, pickup, we decided to give the enemy some smoke and mirrors. We loaded up and began heading to the northernmost point to start there and work our way south but along the way we planned several stops and false dismounts. We proceeded accordingly, stopping to let out 1st Squad, who fanned out to set up security, only to then quickly egress back to the trucks and load up. One of the meaningless actions we took was to stop for five minutes, pop a purple smoke grenade, and speed off rapidly. We intentionally made strategic plans around specific actions that had no purpose whatsoever except to draw the enemy's attention and confuse them. After our final gimmick, we made our way to our last drop point but ran into a Recon convoy on the way who had been trying to locate some enemy fighters that had taken long shots at them. We attached ourselves to the back of their convoy and followed suit. A couple of their snipers dismounted the convoy and climbed up on a steep hillside to the east of the 611 for vantage. They walked through and posted up in a dense, rock-piled graveyard, which was the last place the insurgents would plant IEDs given how badly it would anger the locals. While they scanned the valley, we put the GBOS up in the air and did the same. After some time with no results, they pushed on and we continued our final IED inspections and then RTB (return to base).

DOWNWARD SPIRAL

It was now early April. The weather was perfect, and the poppy flowers and other crops were in full bloom. I didn't expect Sangin to be as beautiful as it turned out to be. It was an oasis in the middle of a mountainous desert filled with beautiful agricultural life. The beauty was easy to overlook but it really did make each day more enjoyable in a uniquely calming way.

Major Wood, our Alpha Company Commander, and Gunny Colman ventured up to PB Alcatraz with us for a few days and rolled right into missions with us. One patrol we went on consisted mostly of road security and because we had Major Wood with us, we made extra stops to engage with some of the local elders. It was not unusual for us to stop and chat with the locals, but we generally stayed out of the more intentional politicking given our small size and limited mission focus. With Major Wood we could not get away with our typical stoicism as his habit for conversational engagement was next level.

Wood took command of Alpha Company just ahead of the start of our deployment work up. It didn't take long for anyone in the company to get to know and admire him because he made it his mission to know every Marine in his command personally on some level. He was an intentional leader, and he didn't shy back from engaging in the work that he had his Marines doing. He was always encouraging, very approachable, and always smiling. His and Gunny's presence was a morale boost for sure and gave us the chance to showcase all that we were doing in the northern valley.

2nd Squad was up for the next foot patrol, and we devised our plan. We were going back into the green zone with the same general mission intent but this time we would make our way deeper in than we had ever gone before. Major Wood let LT continue to steer the ship and he assumed the role of Ramirez's A-gunner, carrying a couple of hundred rounds of ammo belts around his neck on patrol like a salty Vietnam War Marine. We prepared for the patrol just like every other, checking weapons, gear and personnel as well as rehearsing the planned sequence of operations and various contingencies should our course take unexpected turns.

We pushed out from PB Alcatraz at 1030 and headed to the 610N. On arrival 2nd Squad dismounted and we made our way across the IED threat zone, and then inserted into the green zone. Our aim was to make it to a second tree line that resided roughly 300m in. The particular location we inserted included a thick maze of compounds with the main wadi and dense vegetation snaking through them right off the road. Pretty confident in the general characteristics of our surroundings, I led us into the maze. The close proximity of everything made for good cover and concealment but there were also plenty of choke points and the narrow avenues we were forced through made for dangerous enemy machine gun lanes, where a shooter could smoke all of us in one heavy burst if timed right. We made our way into the maze with great caution, moving and covering, staying highly alerted and avoiding as much of the potential danger as we could. The locals fled to the east and M started picking up ICOM chatter. The enemy was on us and starting to coordinate their attack. They were communicating the size of our force, our location, and their own various intended fighting positions. We made it ever so far through the maze and came to a choke point forcing us across a small narrow bridge. Having been warned with obnoxious constancy to never cross small narrow bridges in choke points, I dropped us down into the wadi and began wading upstream. The water was up to our chests in some places, but we were able to continue through it. Thick vinery lined both banks of the narrow wadi amidst other thick, lush crepe myrtle-like trees. There were blind spots all around us, and while safe from pressure plates in the wadi, the water depth and current were really immobilizing, and we needed to get out of it. After a few minutes, I cleared the first line of buildings and climbed the wadi wall posting up on the bank to scan a crop field in front of me to cross. M continued to report on the enemy's attack preparations, and we stayed alert. It could all kick off at any moment.

Once others in the patrol caught up and covered me, I got up and started across the field. We were surrounded by good attack positions, and I was very exposed. All around us were dead spots that could easily conceal one or more of the new snipers we'd been warned about. I walked very cautiously across the field at the ready shifting my aim back and forth from one potential enemy shooting position to the next, taking easy steps, controlling my breathing and staying well postured for a quick engagement. Making it to the other end of the field, I hit another choke point. I looked back toward LT to check for any changes in intent. He gave me an affirming nod to continue, so I advanced and took us right back into the wadi, this time though in a wider and shallower section. We were now far enough into the green zone that we lost sight of both the 611 and our gun trucks and we were behind several rows of buildings. This was new. The wadi straightened out in a long stretch running north–south and gave us an extensive, wide-angled view west. M alerted us that the enemy attack was imminent, so I set up in the middle of the straight run up on the bank of the wadi positioned to cover the rest of the squad as others moved past me and set up to my right.

While the other Marines were working their way into good fighting positions, I noticed one enemy fighter setting up from a semi-concealed position behind a compound wall to my two o'clock. I sighted in on him and then noticed another just a few yards away from him in a thicket of trees and other foliage. They were getting ready to hit us. The radio chatter began to intensify, so we held steady to prepare for the opening bursts of their attack. Most of the civilians had already moved east but there were still a few stragglers clearing the area. Peck set up on my left with Lt Huff, Turner and M to the left of him. Mathes, Gil and Hernandez were set on my right and the rest were spread throughout. More enemy shooters sounded off on their ICOM radios, noting their fighting positions to one another. They were also reaffirming our position and numbers. I called out locations of the combatants I could make out to the rest of the squad and stayed fixed on the two I identified in my sector of fire. LT gave Command a heads-up to start the ordnance process. M was close enough to me that I could hear the Taliban chatter on his green gear radio while he listened in. Their tone was nervous but aggressive. We were waiting for them to start the engagement but could see some of them maneuvering positions on us. I watched the shooter in the tree line slowly moving in and out of view. He was trying to remain covered and concealed enough, while keeping us in his sight. I don't think he knew I could see him.

The civilians were now out of the immediate area and the pressure was building. Awaiting the inevitable fight, I requested permission to take out the shooter in the tree line. LT was tied up on the radio with Command when I made the request and I waited. I eventually made the request again, 'LT, permission to fire?' A few seconds later he responded, 'Affirmative Longgrear, smoke him.' I flipped my safety to fire and began to slow my breathing while waiting for the combatant to come back into view. It was a roughly 200-yard shot, which was not a difficult distance but it was with a heavy heartbeat. Thoughts began to flood my mind. I had experienced enough enemy engagement at this point to satisfy my youthful Marine desire to simply participate in combat, but I had yet to have the enemy squarely in my sights like this. I felt the height of dominating power and the pending fulfilment of that week's build-up of aggression, but it was intertwined with some sense of heartache. As I steadied my breathing, waiting for the combatant to creep back in sight, the burden got heavier.

By now the rest of the squad was well positioned covering various sectors of fire and aimed in on the likely attack positions in front of us. Through the crops and trees obstructing my line of sight I focused intently, trying to identify body mass. Suddenly, my right eye caught movement through thick crop stocks near the location I had last seen the combatant. This was it. I quickly aligned my red ACOG chevron (scope crosshairs), began applying trigger pressure and started my exhale. As my shot was just about to ring out, the combatant's body mass cleared the crop stocks that were obstructing my view, and I rapidly released the trigger without firing while a surge of adrenaline coursed through my body. My eyes widened at the realization that the movement I locked onto was not a combatant but a small boy that could not have been five years' old yet. He was all alone and started running east, trying to clear the area before the fighting started. It had already been several minutes since the last group of civilians left the green zone and this was very unusual. The kids were always the first ones to clear the area as their parents knowingly directed them to safety before the adults. I don't know how or why, but this little boy had been left behind and I was just 2lbs of trigger pressure away from mistakenly killing him. My heart sunk deep into my chest, and I dropped my head into the dirt. I almost just shot a little boy. I called out the child to the rest of the squad so no one else would make the same mistake and started to brush off the angst.

As I regained my composure, I sighted back into the same thicket and moments later the combatant tiptoed back into view. I lined him up quickly and restarted the process. 'Relax your body; slow your breathing; apply trigger pressure; exhale.' I waited and focused intently for the right shot while he slowly crept, positioning himself carefully behind one tree and then another peering towards us and positioning himself to attack. He stayed partially covered. If I waited any longer, he might disappear behind the adjacent compound wall again, and I would miss the chance to take him out of the fight. The weight of the situation bore down on me heavily, and especially after having just narrowly avoided shooting an innocent child. I had a feeling of excitement in making the kill and at the same time felt somewhat ashamed by that excitement. Trying to pull myself out of the mental mix-up with no time to process my feelings, I went numb, zeroed in on center mass, and squeezed. The single shot ripped through the valley and landed. The enemy combatant didn't instantly collapse from the green-tip 5.56mm round but appeared to have taken the hit and slumped over. Immediately after my shot, M heard one of the enemy fighters ask over their radios if the combatant was alright. Then the other enemy fighters went wide open on us.

Heavy gunfire rained in from a sizable murder hole at our ten o'clock, creating a big dust cloud that several of us locked onto. With our attention drawn left, another fighter with an RPG on his shoulder popped out around a corner 15yds away from the combatant I shot. As Mathes saw and turned to shoot him, the combatant let off the RPG before Mathes could pull his trigger. The rocket-propelled grenade screamed toward Mathes and Gil, who dove for cover. It flew right over their heads and exploded into the compound wall behind us. Then several other enemy fighting positions sounded off and rounds were incoming from all over the place. The enemy volume was very heavy on this one. Peck screamed, 'ROCKET UP!!!' He retracted into the wadi and prepped the LAW rocket he was carrying, then took aim at the RPK position at our ten o'clock, putting me slightly in his back blast zone, which could kill me if hit directly. He screamed, 'ROCKET OUT!' I dove into the water away from Peck and hugged the wadi embankment almost entirely submerged when WHAM! I was angled off enough, but caught some of the back blast, which slammed into me and sent me into a daze. Raddled, I got up to look for the impact location but was too dizzy to see across the field. Peck affirmed in anger that the round landed just short of a direct hit, but it did send the machine gunner running. Peck tossed the spent rocket tube and re-engaged with his M4. My daze subsided moments later and I looked down the line of the berm to see our squad engaging in full force. Mathes and Hernandez were lobbing 203s over the compound walls and into doorways that shooters were engaging from, Gil and Blair were clamoring their SAWs in talking guns fashion and

Ramirez was chipping away at the murder holes with the M240G. LT and Turner were coordinating with Command for aerial support. We were guns blazing and the rounds were whistling, cracking and ricocheting in all directions. At any given point, an enemy shooter would have his shots tuned in almost just right, pelting the berm in front of one of us and forcing us down into the wadi, to reposition in one direction or another. It was an all-out engagement.

Before long the incoming rounds slowed down. We had gained the initiative and started backing off on our rate of fire. M screamed out that several of the enemy fighters were hit and the rest were losing confidence as he listened to their commander bark out orders that the fighters refused to follow.

Sometime later, we slowed to a brief ceasefire to assess the situation. It got quiet enough for a moment to hear far off. Coming from behind the compound wall directly in front of me were the belting moans of a dying man in what sounded like excruciating pain. There was no way to know which one of us hit him. He whelped and cried for thirty seconds and then his cries started to die down. I pitied the man in that moment. It was hard to listen to. His screams eventually subsided after what I assume to have been his bleeding out and things became very still. Air support was on the way at this point, but the opposition was no longer forceful, and we called them off. Several of us wanted to secure the compounds that the enemy fired from but there was no substantiated reason to take the pressure plate risk. Command later affirmed they would send a Recon squad in to hit the compounds and perform dead checks.

We egressed out, slowly making our way out of the wadi while moving and covering for one another. We rounded a large group of mud buildings and crossed the lush crop fields that were between us and the 611. As I crossed the final field to crest the hillside that our trucks were covering us from, I came up on a deep dry wadi with steep embankments. I chose what I thought to be the best avenue down but slipped. When I did, I landed on a shrub stock that had been hacked off at a 45° and it punctured straight through my pants and into the back of my left leg. I rolled off it into the trench and yelled out in pain. Reaching back to identify the wound, it didn't appear to be as bad as the pain first suggested but I had a 1in puncture wound in the back of my leg. Peck helped me up the other embankment and crest the hillside along the 611. We loaded into the trucks with 1st Squad and RTB.

On the way back to Alcatraz the mood was ecstatic, but I was bitter. We leveled our enemy's attack again and left unscathed, but this one got to me. Hearing the whelping moans of the dying enemy fighter, complete silence in the aftermath of apparently killing some of the other combatants, acknowledging how close I was to accidentally shooting a little boy, and grappling with a growing resentment of our enemy, really sank me. I was embattled internally. As much as I tried to stay disconnected and just do my job, things started to get personal. It seemed that way for a lot of us and I don't know realistically how anyone could do any different in the circumstances.

Growing up, I often heard of the 'innocence lost' for warfighters who returned home without the spark of life that they had before leaving. All of us managed wartime pressures in our own ways. I did not anticipate the emotional storm of it all, at least not in some of the ways I experienced it. There was a real exhilaration in fighting and killing, especially after undergoing the violent Marine Corps indoctrination that I did. At times though it was accompanied by heartache, even in light of the justice being served that undergirded our being there in the first place. I just disdained the loss of life and general human suffering. After many of the enemy encounters I walked away from, I felt both accomplished and conflicted to some extent. The more I thought about it at any given time, the worse it got. The best thing to do was to try to retract from the emotion, become numb and not think deeply about any of it. That is not how God hardwired me though and I often thought deep into all of it. There's a song lyric about war from an artist named Zack Hemsey that says,

'He holds his rifle to his chest, his heart is heavy with regret as he unloads with his offence, and "in the name of freedom" is chanted to loud applause, while planted in his brain is an image of hell crossed. Sobbing in his spirit and fearing the holocaust, He must compose himself or risk being the next lost ...' There may not be words that better describe how I felt at times than these, which highlight the convoluted nature of taking part in combat. I knew when I joined the Marines that my participation in war would likely come with higher costs than I could foresee. I had no regrets then, nor will I ever for choosing to bear war's burdens on behalf of a greater good, but it was messy. It was not easy to manage then, and those burdens are still at times difficult to live with now.

When we got back to Alcatraz, I stripped my gear, cleaned my weapon, debriefed with the team, and then got alone for a while. Of all the things I contended with overseas, keeping my heart from hardening with hatred was one of my biggest internal struggles. I spent time in prayer laying my burdens at the feet of Jesus, who himself voluntarily bore the burdens of humanity for the greatest good. 'Father God, thank you for helping me through another day. Please Father, don't let me lose myself. Protect my heart from growing cold and give me grace to love the way you do. Forgive me for the vengeance I harbor in my heart. God help me to navigate all this in a way that honors you.' All throughout the deployment I did everything I could to be intentional and effective as a fighter but to never let hatred or blood lust stay rooted in me. It was all just a job that someone had to do. That's what I told myself anyway.

> *'War brings forward the best and worst of humanity, but mostly worst.'*
>
> Landon Longgrear

Chapter 7

THE TIPPING POINT

'War is love, devotion and heroism beautifully painted across a canvas of cruelty.'

Landon Longgrear

With the acceleration of good weather and blooming vegetation came a heightened intensity in the enemy's attacks. Since the move to Alcatraz, we encountered enemy activity in some capacity almost every time we went outside the wire. We were all now well acquainted with our daily realities and the topics of injury and death became increasingly trivial. We had not been significantly impacted yet by either, so it was easy to feel that way. Even on the days we remained at Alcatraz, explosions and gunfire sounded off in the distance as Recon squads were in and out of their own combat incursions. I doubt there was ever a single day in the valley that was completely docile after the Marines arrived.

On the evening of April 3, we huddled up to discuss our next patrol. 2nd Squad would be on foot and 1st in the trucks. Our plan was to drop two teams into separate locations in the green zone in the early dark morning. We would be roughly 500m apart and set up to study the local environment during sunrise, looking for suspicious behavior and things out of place. We would then patrol toward the other team along the main wadi in search of command wires and

Marine Corps Bootcamp Lima Company Platoon 3242 final parade deck march on graduation day led by Platoon Honorman, Private First Class Longgrear.

On far left Longgrear and other 2nd Platoon Marines on cold, rainy field training evolution at Camp Pendleton during pre-deployment workup.

Left to right: Greer & Rast ahead of a night mission during the "Final Exercise" of our pre-deployment workup.

Alpha Company Marines in the belly of a C17 enroute to Afghanistan.

Left: Boots on the ground at FOB Nolay in Sangin, Helmand Province, after helo drop off.

Below: One of several unit Command Posts at FOB Nolay in Sangin. MRAP truck with a mine roller on the right. MATVs on the left.

Above: One of many IED explosions in the green zone just outside the perimeter of FOB Nolay in early spring 2011.

Right: Left to right: Mathes, Flemming, Apgar, and Longgrear pit-stopped at FOB Jackson. 6x6 MRAP with mounted 50cal in the turret.

Tattered remains of the 6x6 MRAP that was blown off Route 611 during 2nd Platoon's first patrol outside the wire.

Sangin Bazaar, the most modern area in the region.

Ashley investigating a possible IED on Route 611.

A father's affirmation.

Above left: Marine Corps Super Stallion helo dust off after resupply drop off.

Above right: Garcia and his mangled truck after his late night IED strike on Route 611. Longgrear, Ashley, and others attempting to mount a spare wheel and tire ahead of journeying back south to FOB Nolay in the middle of the night.

Battle Squad. Full 2nd Squad at Patrol Base Alcatraz ahead of combat patrol into the enemy-held northern Sangin Valley green zone.

Left: 1st Squad Marines cautiously patrolling up Route 611 anticipating the opening bursts of an enemy ambush. Fresh IED hole to their left.

Below: 6x6 MRAP (with mine roller) serving perimeter security at PB Alcatraz overlooking the green zone. Helmand River in the distance.

Above left: Home away from home. 1st & 2nd Squad's living space at PB Alcatraz right beside the burn pit.

Above right: PB Alcatraz's burn pit.

Longgrear and Mathes gearing up for a night mission.

2nd Squad Marines posted on wadi berm 300 meters into the green zone after squelching a heavy enemy engagement.

Above left: Smith coordinating air support from his truck on Route 611 while 2nd Squad engages in a firefight on foot.

Above right: Greer engaging enemy fighters with the 50 cal from his MRAP turret during an intense ambush on Route 611. Taunting Taliban flags in the field just in front of him.

Above: 1st Squad Marines combat patrol along Route 611. Moving and covering one another against the threat of an enemy attack.

Left: HIMARS rocket drop on an enemy position during a 2nd Platoon gunbattle.

Above left: Garcia scanning the green zone after beating back an enemy attack.

Above right: Longgrear at PB Alcatraz mounting up to taxi 1st Squad to their drop location for foot patrol.

Right: Purple smoke popped in the vicinity of an IED location on Route 611.

Below: Ashley and Turner posted along a wadi berm monitoring the green zone after combating an enemy small arms attack.

1st Squad Marines loaded in the back of the 6x6 MRAP to be dropped off for combat patrol.

Above: Enemy bullet impact on Gil's M249 SAW during the first burst of an enemy ambush. Very close call.

Left: Smith returning to the truck from the green zone after crossing the main wadi.

Left to right: (Sniper team) Stevens, Staffen, Hahn, and Flemming at PB Alcatraz ahead of combat patrol into the green zone.

1st and 2nd Squads of Alpha Company, 1/23 inside the meager walls of PB Alcatraz just ahead of a ground battle with enemy fighters.

Above left: Little girl clutching a baby and making her way east through a beautiful poppy field to clear the green zone ahead of an enemy ambush. Other local civilians follow behind her.

Above right: Gil observing the green zone in early civil twilight.

Right: Longgrear scanning for enemy shooters after a firefight lull.

Above: Finnern & Ashley watching for remaining combatants across an open poppy field after a HIMARS rocket drop on an enemy fighting position.

Left: Wood and Ashley laughing in the back of the 6x6 MRAP after having fought their way through an enemy ambush on foot.

Peaceful sunset ahead of a night patrol.

Top: Evacuating Smith and Rast.

Above: 1st and 2nd Squads walking away from a debrief at PB Alcatraz the day Smith and Rast were killed.

Right: A warrior's monument posted at FOB Jackson.

Longgrear on mounted patrol along Route 611.

Above left: Staffen covering other Marines as they egress to the trucks after patrol.

Above right: Infrared screen view of Marines checking possible IEDs on Route 611 in the middle of the night.

Left: Lighthearted heavy weapons cleaning. (Left to right: Greer, Longgrear, Mathes, Garcia)

Right: 1st and 2nd Squads arrive at FOB Delaram for the first time.

Below: Mathes and Longgrear departing for a night mission outside of Delaram.

3rd Squad's burning truck from IED direct hit outside of Delaram.

Final view of IED infested Route 611 and blood stained poppy fields of the northern Sangin Valley green zone.

pressure plates and regroup somewhere in the middle. One nuance to this patrol was that my team would be inserting into the green zone near the location we extracted from during our first gun battle, and we would be patrolling south basically in reverse, which felt a little hair-raising. We prepped our gear and turned in for the night. When 0230 rolled around we geared up, did self-checks, buddy checks, and gear checks. At 0330 we loaded into the trucks and at 0400 we pushed.

1st Squad dropped my team a couple of hundred meters north of the 610N and Ashley's at the 605N, 500m south. I led us down the 611 quietly and cautiously, scanning surroundings through my NVGs while listening intently for any threat indications. Reaching our insertion point, I made my way in, nervously crossing the IED threat zone along the side of the 611, which was somewhere in the vicinity of the IED near miss I had on our first patrol in that area. We trudged through despite our low visibility and made it across intact. We quietly traversed passed a group of compounds, crossed a tree line, and dropped down into a thigh-high wheat patch that lined the main wadi overlooking the green zone on the other side. I laid down in the prone and fixed my focus on two compounds 100m across the poppy field in front of me. Once we were all concealed, things got very quiet and still. The sound of the wadi's gentle waterflow backdropped brief gusts of wind rustling the trees and chirps of early-morning insects. It was all calm, but we were alert.

In less than an hour the early civil twilight began. Several minutes later a teenaged boy appeared out of nowhere and approached the other side of the wadi. He was fiddling around with no real purpose and posed no threat. He could not see us, but we were just 30m away watching him. Mathes picked up a small rock and threw it into the water when the boy was not looking. The boy shot around alerted, trying to figure out what created the splash. After a moment he shrugged it off and turned his back again, at which time Mathes threw another rock into the water. This time when the boy turned around, he knew something was up and began intently scanning to discover the culprit. Unable to identify what or who was responsible, a look of nervous concern came on his face, and he hurriedly headed back to his compound. I quietly laughed and motioned an air pound over to Mathes. It was the perfect shenanigan for the moment.

For the next twenty minutes, the locals slowly began to emerge out of their compounds, all shaking off their slumber as they began their morning routines. A woman dressed in all black emerged from one of the compounds across the first field and began slowly making her way right toward us down a well-beaten dirt path that split a beautiful vibrant-colored poppy field. We were well concealed but not enough that she would not notice us if she continued along that path, which lined the northern edge of the wheat patch we were in. She eventually crossed the wadi and continued right toward us. It appeared the wheat patch we were in was actually her wheat patch. What a surprise she was in for. As she got right to the edge she looked up and her eyes opened wide in shock to several muzzles pointed right at her. We didn't know what she was going to do. She let out a loud fearful shriek, took a step back somewhat frozen and then hurriedly turned back toward her compound. Everyone in earshot became alerted and watched her dart back across the field. A couple minutes later waves of civilians began leaving the green zone, kids first, and many along the same path right beside us. We scanned each of them carefully from a distance through our ACOGs, adults especially, for weapons as they approached us, ensuring none of them tried to pull a fast one and surprise attack us as they walked by. Several MAMs remained behind though, staring us down. I remember one specifically leaned up against a doorway, calm and collected but mean, mugging us hard. He stood there flexing while the others fled. We stood up straight and locked eyes glaring right back at him as if to taunt one another prior to the obvious upcoming engagement.

The sun had now cleared the horizon and with the civilian flow trickling, we began south as the MAMs disappeared behind the compounds. M was having radio problems and struggled to pick up

ICOM, but the stage was already set. I continued leading the patrol south on the east side of the wadi through thick trees and eventually came to a pinch point that required us scaling over a chest-high wall. There was no good way around it to our east and it bordered the wadi to the west, which at this location involved an unusually high and steep embankment. Scaling a dirt wall this tall in all our combat gear was not easy and made me think of all the early training we did in boot camp on this very thing. I made it over the wall first and moved 20m forward from it, posting security to cover the rest of the guys. Peck followed, then LT and then Turner. When Turner came over the wall and landed, he rolled his ankle badly and fell over on the ground. LT tried to get Turner up, but he struggled to put any weight on his ankle. This placed us in a bad position given an attack was fast approaching. Our team had only seven Marines and half were still on the other side of the wall. Turner was on the ground with no cover and struggling to move while LT was equally exposed tending to him.

We called the trucks to pick up Turner while the rest of the team hurriedly came over the wall. Garcia made it over and joined me in the front while I moved further south to give us more dispersion. I laid down in the prone at the wadi edge and started scanning the compounds across the first poppy field through my ACOG, panning right to left. All of a sudden, what looked like a forty-year-old thick-bearded man in brown tactical fatigues slowly rounded the outer corner of a building. I put him in my crosshairs immediately. His eyes were fixated on the rest of the team scaling the wall and he did not notice that I had him squarely in my sights. He didn't have a weapon in hand but was wearing a black chest rig of sorts and had a radio up to his mouth reporting to his team on our situation. I disconcerted myself on what to do. This man was obviously an enemy combatant, maybe even a commander, but he was presenting no weapon, shots had not yet been fired and our ICOM hack was down, meaning positive identification in its strictest sense could be argued. If I killed him and he turned out not to be a validated enemy combatant, I could be criminally charged, according to that snarky JAG attorney, even though this man was very apparently taking part in coordinating an attack on us. LT and now Peck were still dealing with Turner, and I was too far forward to get their attention for approval to engage. It also occurred to me that if I took the shot, it may kick off the firefight on both sides and my team was still very exposed. I was perfectly confident I could eliminate the one enemy fighter, but his buddies might get LT, Peck and Turner in a quick rebuttal. I began squeezing my trigger, but then released; and then again; and then I finally conceded not to take the shot. A deep frustration came on me like I just let a criminal go free. Restraint seemed like the right decision in that situation, but it angered me deeply.

The combatant eventually disappeared back behind the compound and did not appear again. I lost my chance to take him out, but it gave LT and Peck enough time to get Turner up off the ground and out of the open before the shooting started. The roadside was not too far uphill from our location, and they got Turner up to it and loaded into one of the two 1st Squad trucks that had dropped us off hours prior. With Turner on board, the trucks reassumed their positions north of us on the road to cover our flank. Mathes and Gil, who brought up the rear of the patrol, made it over the wall and when LT and Peck came back down the hill we got up and continued pushing south. In what seemed like no more than a minute after we picked up and began to move south again, the attack began. The enemy let loose and this time they were accurate. The first volley sent incoming rounds ricocheting off the ground right in front of my feet and snapping right past me. I jumped like firecrackers were just thrown down at my toes and broke for the nearest cover but ended up behind a very skinny tree right on the edge of the wadi and I was very exposed. I braced the tree and began engaging left to right to suppress for the rest of the squad to find cover. I was in a bad a position and my adrenaline was surging. Shifting fire from one likely enemy shooting position to the next, I emptied one mag, dropped it from the mag well, slammed another one in and kept ripping. I heard Peck screaming out from somewhere in the distance behind me amidst the gun fire, 'LONGGREAR!!' I turned and saw the rest of the squad hunkered down in a dry wadi ditch 20m away. I made eye contact with Peck, who gave me the nod and then started laying down cover fire for me. As soon as he did, I sprinted back and dove in. At this point we were all wide open trying to gain fire superiority. Incoming rounds were raining in, hitting the ground in front of us, wisping and snapping close overhead and pelting the embankment that our backs were against. It felt like we were getting shot at from every direction but behind us and directly south. Various automatic weapons were sounding off and overlapping while deep, single-shot sniper rifle pitches rung out intertwined. The enemy was in compound positions to our south-west and west and in tree lines to our north. They came to play that day and their aim was dialed in. They had us pinned down and they were initially out-gunning us in volume. We were all shooting and bobbing while our gunfire and the enemy's ebbed and flowed. As with most of the firefights, after the initial exchange the shooting would have moments of great intensity, and then slow down to a brief lull, and then ramp right back up again.

Garcia was just on the other side of Peck from me. Quickly into the engagement, a sniper zeroed in on him. While his head was barely cresting the berm, a bullet came in and landed right in front of his face by just inches, blowing enough rock and debris into his eyes that his eye pro were scarred up beyond use. Just a couple of inches higher and it would have been lights out for Garcia. He laid low in what happened to be a shallow part of the ditch and I watched and listened to round after round come in every two seconds as if on cadence hitting the exact same spot, chipping away the dirt that provided him with cover. He stayed as low as he could, trying not to get shot, and yelled out, 'THEY HAVE PID ON ME! THEY HAVE PID ON ME!' (Positive Identification). I screamed back, 'KEEP YOUR HEAD DOWN! WE'LL GET HIM!' Peck and I anxiously tried to locate the shooter. The longer we scanned for him the quicker the incoming rounds seemed to refocus to us though, forcing us right back down.

The 611 was at the top of the steep embankment at our backs and the same two trucks that picked up Turner came back to our position quickly after the firing started. The lead truck had a 50 cal in the turret and it stopped right above me on the road and began firing directly over my head. I was on the muzzle end of the most powerful-caliber weapon we had at our disposal, and the concussion that came out of the barrel with each round was so overwhelming that I struggled to function while it fired, even 40-50m or more away from it and at a lower elevation. It raddled my brain and hurt my ears so bad that all I could do was crouch down and clinch my body with my hands over my ears and wait for it to stop firing. It was painfully disabling. After the 50 cal's third burst, I started crawling further south down the ditch to get away from the muzzle path.

Now a good stretch away from the rest of the squad, I affixed my focus to our south–south-west flank, given I was the furthest in that direction. As the truck turret gunners pounded the enemy positions, we gained fire superiority and incoming rounds began to trickle. Soon after, LT had a HIMARS rocket on its way. It was danger close at 150m. The minimum safe distance for a HIMARS is 200-plus. LT yelled that impact was seconds out and we hunkered down. Every time we called in ordnance it was a nervous event. Just a number or two off on a coordinate could result in bringing the bomb down right on top of us and once they are in the air there is nothing anyone can do to stop it. We braced and the rocket slammed into one of the compounds we were taking fire from right across the first crop field in front of us, sending an enormous fireball and thick black smoke cloud into the air. It shook everything and immediately halted all the gunfire. We checked ourselves, checked each other, reloaded, and repositioned. Mathes came up to the front of the patrol and Peck moved in more centrally. We re-established sectors of fire and scanned the battlefield.

When we initially came under fire, LT called up the other team to double-time it to reinforce us. They began to hustle in our direction, weaving in and out of the main wadi but started taking fire and they too got pinned down. They stayed put during the HIMARS drop and covered the southern flank, which squirters were likely to egress through. While two of the 1st Squad trucks came to our support, the other two went to theirs.

At some point during the battle we had an ISR drone come online. While we were engaged in the firefight, the drone oversaw the battlefield and tracked the enemy combatants that we couldn't see. Between that and 1st Squad listening into the enemy's ICOM in the trucks, we had them locked down. After the HIMARS hit, the surviving enemy fighters communicated that they were going to collect their dead, so we stuck around to take out the rest. They made their movements out of our sight on the ground but not out of view from our trucks or the ISR drone. A few minutes into waiting, one of the trucks spotted a combatant trying to sneak into the area and the turret gunner on the road let out two M240G bursts that dropped him in place. The ISR drone tracked others who were moving south. After maybe thirty more minutes of waiting, we were ordered to RTB. Team-2 made our way up the steep embankment at our backs and loaded into the two gun-trucks to regroup with the others. As we loaded up, Team-1 began egressing to their trucks also but just as they got to the roadside orders came in that we were to re-engage the enemy. The ISR drone watched as the enemy fighters consolidated in a specific mosque that we identified as being 200m south-west of Ashley's position and roughly the same distance west of the 611.

Team-2 beelined south to link up with the other trucks ahead of our next engagement. We made it to the others and all four trucks started positioning for an attack on the enemy's consolidation. By the time we in the trucks got set, Team-1 was back down at the wadi and further south. As they were each getting into their fighting positions, a PKM burst ripped open and rounds impacted right between Major

Wood's upper thighs as he lay leaning up against the wadi berm nearly tagging him in the last place a man wants to get shot. He quickly rolled into another covered position as the other Team-1 Marines returned fire. Immediately after the guys on the ground returned fire at the enemy shooter inside the mosque, we launched our attack from the turrets. SSgt Smith's truck had our Mk19 auto grenade launcher in the turret and his gunner began unloading HE (high-explosive) grenades right through a door opening facing us on the 611, sending squirters out the sides and back of the building, where our other turret gunners were positioned to mow them down with the M240Gs and 50 cal. The ISR drone monitored the engagement and tracked some of the combatants that exited the rear of the building out of our view from the road, who then made their way south into other adjacent compounds. Command lined up another HIMAS fire mission and dropped a second HIMARS rocket right on top of them. The offensive didn't last long and when it all came to a lull, we had let lose more than one hundred Mk19 HE grenades, hundreds of M240G rounds and an additional HIMARS rocket. At the end of it, we held in place for thirty minutes scanning for any further ICOM chatter and staying positioned to engage any additional enemy movement the ISR drone picked up. No more enemy activity arose.

Preceding our attack, M had identified the names of three Taliban leaders that had been coordinating attacks on us in the weeks prior. Not only did we take out a number of fighters, but we were convinced that we managed to take out all three of those main leaders. Overall, this firefight was the closest any of us had come to being hit ourselves. When my team loaded up in the trucks, Gil showed us the bipod on his SAW, which had taken a bullet while he was running for cover during the opening bursts of the initial ambush; that same wave of incoming rounds that nearly punched my time clock at the front of the patrol element. Even with the close calls, this was probably the most successful mission so far given the number of enemy combatants and unit commanders we eliminated without any casualties on our end.

When we got back to Alcatraz I got out of the truck, and someone noticed that one of the view windows up in one of the 50 cal turrets had taken a bullet impact. We all went to congratulate the gunner on skirting death, and someone went up close and noticed that the round had impacted on the inside of the turret rather than the outside. Immediately questioning how this happened, everyone looked at the gunner, whose face became coy ... during the fight his 50 cal jammed up and he began engaging with his M16, which he then accidentally shot his turret window with, ha ha! It could have easily happened to any of us, but we gave him a hard time about it anyway.

One of our Battalion sniper teams was at Alcatraz waiting for us when we got back, which was overdue and welcomed. Being as thin-manned as we were, we had been requesting our other 2nd Platoon squad to be relieved of their Jump Mission in Delaram and come to our support in Sangin. Our Battalion Commander could not make that happen given they were attached to Regimental Command, who wouldn't part with them, but he did finally send us a sniper team. We spent the evening dialing them into everything in preparation for our patrol the following day. With the distance dynamics of our firefights so far, we felt they would prove to be very effective. We all huddled up for LT's Warning Order for our next patrol and then went into the evening routine of cleaning weapons, performing truck maintenance, preparing gear, and rehearsing our next patrol sequence before racking out under the stars, all still beside our perpetually smoldering toxic burn pit.

EVERYONE PAYS THE PIPER IN SANGIN

April 6, 2011, kicked off up tempo. We woke up and mission briefed first thing. 2nd Squad would taxi 1st to the 630N, where they would dismount and foot patrol into the green zone, endeavoring to accomplish our typical enemy and IED identification and elimination, and then extract at the 619N. We prepped and checked gear, loaded up and pushed out at 0700. As we drove north, we ran into several locations on the 611 that were heavily tampered with. The enemy had been busy the night before. There were what appeared to be intentional false flags everywhere and in total way more than we had seen on any given day before. It was almost like they were responding to our mission method hoaxes with their own. Trash and fabric were hung all along the roadside. Rocks were turned up on their sides and in two locations there were daisy chains of big rocks strung all the way across the road. I suspect these locations were intended to stop us long enough for spotters to give the ambush teams up the road a heads-up that we were on the way so they could get set up before we reached their intended kill zone. We did a quick IED search at each spot and then continued pushing.

As we neared our mission's insertion point, an IED blast cap exploded right under the 6x6 just as Garcia (driver) and Mathes passed over it. They felt the blast right underneath them, which was supposed to ignite the ammonium nitrate that the actual IED was comprised of, but it failed to, thank God. This was a near direct hit and would have been catastrophic. The 6x6 was our main casevac truck, our largest troop carrier and was generally positioned in the middle of the convoy. In this instance, because we were transporting our foot patrol element with the addition of our new sniper team, the truck was completely packed. If the IED had ignited, it would have taken out Mathes, Garcia, Flemming, Apgar and six of the 1st Squad Marines who were loaded up in it for dismount. It also would have split our convoy in half. We just barely skirted a very serious mass casualty situation.

As fate would have it, our planned insertion point was just ahead of where the failed IED attempt took place. Being right in the kill zone of the intended enemy ambush, we pushed up the road just a little further, making sure our trucks cleared the IED, and then quickly dismounted 1st Squad, who fanned out to set up security to the west while the trucks established sectors of fire in all directions. Me, Peck and Ramirez were in the second to last truck of the convoy and had a good view of 1st Squad's initial push into the green zone. Ashley, Blair, and Gil were in the rear truck behind us, LT, Turner and Hernandez were in the lead truck and Garcia, Mathes, Flemming and Apgar were in the second truck. I suspect our dismount threw the intended ambush off (no more so than the failed IED strike), which delayed their opening shots, but within minutes of the dismount, the enemy was weapons free, and we were receiving enemy rounds on and off from every direction but south. This time the enemy fighters had set up a U-shape ambush of sorts comprised of several fighting positions in the west and north and an IDF (indirect fire, or artillery mortars) team in the hills to our east. Rounds started coming in from the west and north, and not long after mortars came down at our trucks from the east. My truck and Ashley's were sandwiched between compounds that closely lined the 611. Me and Peck were watching the avenues of approach to ensure no one snuck up close to RPG or grenade us. At the same time, we were scurrying to identify the mortar locations for Ramirez in the turret to engage. Maneuvering the truck around for vantage, we got Ramirez locked on to one of the mortar positions and he let loose. Gil was the turret gunner in the rear truck and maintained security of our six while the gunners in the two lead trucks focused on our front and covering the foot patrol element to the west. 1st Squad was eventually dispersed widely throughout the compounds, fields, and trenches in between the 611 and the main wadi trying to locate and eliminate enemy shooters in the green zone. Our snipers were intertwined in the foot patrol element and were doing their best to pick off the enemy fighters from a distance. This was our first engagement with precision reach, and it made an impact. In one instance Sgt Hahn, with our integrated sniper team, tagged an enemy combatant as they got up to move fighting positions, wounding him critically but not immediately killing him. As the wounded shooter tried to crawl for cover, Hahn stayed focused on him and another enemy fighter picked up to reposition. Hahn dropped the second enemy combatant right behind the first.

The 4x magnified ACOGs that the rest of us had were an enormous improvement from iron sights, but the distance optics and weaponry of the snipers put us on a whole new level of lethality.

As soon as the shooting started, LT began coordinating with command and a ISR Predator drone loaded with Hellfire missiles was sent in to overlook the battlefield. Coordination efforts among the dispersed ground teams, our squad in the trucks, local command elements and a remote drone pilot proved an immense challenge. Amidst the radio traffic, the order eventually came over for the guys on the ground to consolidate as a Hellfire drop was imminent. The furthest inserted team in the green zone went to consolidate back along a wadi that lined the eastern edge of a large crop field. Smith and Rast were pushed further into the green zone than most and held firm in their position to continue providing cover for the other Marines. The radio traffic was heavy. MAMs were scattered throughout the area, and we were taking sporadic gunfire from numerous locations. LT made his way on the radio amidst the traffic and yelled, 'BREAK, BREAK IMPACT IN 17 SECONDS, SAY AGAIN, IMPACT IN 17 SECONDS.' Moments later the explosion ripped through the valley, and I watched from my truck on the 611 the smoke plume clear the treetops to my west in typical fashion. We cheered excitedly, even though the explosion seemed to be closer than it should have been. Quickly after the blast, the ground element came across the radio screaming, 'CEASEFIRE, CEASEFIRE!' with the highest shrill of angst. Our exhilaration immediately halted; this was a very uncharacteristic response to an ordnance drop. Sgt Hammonds then came on with a gut-wrenching transmission, 'BREAK, BREAK, BREAK, THAT LANDED RIGHT ON TOP OF RAST AND SMITH!' Peck and I looked at each other shocked, 'Did he just say what I think he said? LT immediately came on, 'SAY AGAIN YOUR LAST ...' Hammonds replied a few seconds later, 'That dropped ... right on top of Smith and Rast.' We waited helplessly for further communication. One of the Marines on the ground came on the radio, 'Corpsman up!

I need Flemming on my position now!' Doc Flemming and Mathes dismounted from the 6x6 and sprinted to the west, disappearing into the foliage. A short while later what we all feared came across the radio. The ground element requested for immediate medevac followed by two 9-lines, one 'critical' and one 'routine'. We all knew what that meant. If in a casualty situation a Marine was badly wounded but alive with a chance to survive then the communication was 'critical'. Conversely, if a Marine had been killed, there was no rush for the medevac given he was already beyond saving and the communication was 'routine'. One of them was dead and the other not far from it. One of the second squad Marines in the trucks belted out a knee-jerk reaction over the radio, 'WHO IS ROUTINE!?' As if in that moment it mattered … nothing came through, even though we were all thinking the same thing.

Smith and Rast were pushed out just far enough beyond the rest of the patrol element that the drone pilot locked onto them from the get-go. How he did not recognize the fact that they were shooting to the west and not toward us to the east I don't know. In the coordinated effort to identify the enemy and friendly positions for the Hellfire drop, something went awry. Drone pilots are taught that when dropping missiles to take out groups they should focus their aim at an individual in the group rather than splitting the difference. This ensures that at the very least they take out the one combatant rather than potentially only wounding multiple. Smith was the targeted individual. When LT's transmission came through, 'Seventeen seconds to impact,' Smith and Rast took cover in place, never imagining that they were the target, and the Hellfire was coming down right on top of them regardless of where they were. Had they got up to move it likely would not have mattered anyway.

Staff Sergeant Jeremy Smith, our respected Platoon Sergeant, was dead on impact. The missile obliterated his body. Doc Benjamin Rast, our brother and trusted Corpsman, also took a bad portion of the blast. When Flemming and Mathes got on scene, they immediately started working on Rast. He was in critical condition. Shrapnel had showered his body, and he was bleeding from multiple wounds but still had a pulse. They got him into what they thought was a stable enough condition to move and then slid him onto a makeshift stretcher to begin moving him to the trucks. Smith's body was then also loaded onto a stretcher to be carried out. All the Marines not directly engaged in handling Smith and Rast were covering the others, still trying to identify enemy shooters and repel incoming enemy fire. Moving Rast back to the trucks was slow. He had a defensive lineman-type build, the terrain was unforgiving, and the pressure plate threat was as real as any other day. A couple of gunship helos arrived and circled our position as a show of force to help keep the enemy from attacking while the ground element egressed. The enemy continued to attack anyway, but not with the same aggression that they otherwise would have.

When the six Marines carrying Rast eventually cleared the foliage, those of us in the trucks finally got a glimpse of our wounded brothers. We covered our sectors of fire and engaged the enemy's sporadic shots while the recovery team made their way up to the 6x6 with Rast to load him in. They were moving as fast as they could as to avoid catching incoming rounds. The turrets and other Marines in the ground element continued to suppress enemy gunfire while the rest of us did our best to locate and fire on new enemy positions as the enemy fighters maneuvered around us. Not long after Rast was loaded into the truck another group followed behind with Smith. They quickly put him in a body bag and loaded him into the back seat of LT's MATV to give as much room as possible in the 6x6 for Mathes and Flemming to keep working on Rast.

The medevac choppers were already called in but given our continued enemy engagement, our predetermined landing zone was scrapped, and the helos arranged to meet us just outside PB Alcatraz. The remainder of 1st Squad hurriedly egressed back to the trucks. Smith was gone but we thought there was still a chance for Rast.

We raced back to Alcatraz to get Rast on the chopper as soon as possible. Flemming and Mathes worked Rast's unconscious body all the way there. His heartbeat had apparently stopped before they loaded him into the truck, but they tried to get it back while enroute. When we pulled up to Alcatraz, I jumped out of my truck and ran over to LT's to pull Smith's body out. I opened the back door to a person-size thick plastic bag slumped over in the seat and had an immediate reaction of pause as my brain struggled to grasp the situation. I hoisted Smith out of the truck gently and his blood that had pooled in the seat beneath him and congregated in the bottom of the bag splashed up on me and ran down my chest. I was shocked. It was all a little too real. Amidst all the chaos, Turner, who was in the truck turret for the entire event and focused on engaging enemy shooters, had no idea who was in the body bag that had been loaded into the back seat right beside him. When I started to pull Smith's body out of the truck, Turner crouched down through the turret hole and said, 'WHO THE FUCK IS THAT?' I said, 'It's Smith, man.' He immediately burst into tears and sunk back into his turret seat. I carefully laid Smith on a stretcher and ran over to help the other guys offload Rast from the 6x6 just as the Blackhawk medevac chopper approached and touched down, kicking up a thick brown cloud of dust. Six of us picked up Rast and ran him to the helo. I gripped the stretcher in one hand up by Rast's chest and his right hand in my other. His face was turned away from me and I saw that he had a golf ball-size hole behind his right ear that went nearly all the way through the other side of his head. At this point I didn't know we had already lost him but in seeing the gaping cavity in the back of his head I knew things had to be final. I think the saving grace of the event for both Smith and Rast is that they didn't suffer at all. They were gone quick.

Under the thundering sound of the helo's rotation, I leaned in and yelled in Rast's ear, 'Hold on Rast, hold on! The Lord's got you now, hold on!' We slid him on to the chopper and the on-board Corpsman immediately started working him. I ran back and grabbed a hold of

Smith with the others. When we approached the medevac chopper with Smith in the body bag the other on-board Corpsman hand saluted the body before receiving it into the helo. It was heavy and that hand salute sealed it all for me. A rush of emotion came on as my adrenaline dissipated and reality set in. We hoisted Smith's body into the chopper and stepped back to watch them dust off.

Everything slowed down and no one knew what to do or say. I walked over to clean the back seat of the MATV that I had pulled Smith out of. When I opened the door and looked in, I stood there for a moment under the gravity of all that had just transpired, staring at the bloody remains of what was just a little while ago one mountain of a man, now resigned only to memory. This was just a matter of time, and we knew the writing was on the wall for some of us but now that we had finally received our taste of death it felt so surreal. Hahn, from our sniper team, grabbed my shoulder and motioned at me. He looked me in the eyes and said, 'Don't worry about this, I'll take care of it. I got it ... Longgrear I got it.' I walked off and began clearing my weapon. Everyone was in minor shock; no one was saying much of anything. Just subtle tears.

In what seemed like a miracle, while Hammonds was recovering Smith's gear that was strewn out across the blast site, he managed to find Smith's wedding ring, which Smith kept looped onto his watch strap when he patrolled. We would now be able to take it home to Smith's wife, Rachel, who at that point was just hours away from answering a door knock to a Marine in dress blues accompanied by a naval chaplain. Between her and Smith, this was going to be his last deployment and they were going to try for children once he got home. Now it had all been ripped away from her in a moment, halfway around the world, and she didn't even know it yet. I was hit hard with that thought. Even worse, I found out later their wedding anniversary was April 7, the very next day.

How the events of April 6 would all pan out and be looked upon in the days following was questionable. We were caught in an ambush and being attacked from multiple locations, but this was still friendly fire. Smith and Rast were not killed by enemy rounds or IEDs but by our own Hellfire missile. We huddled up to debrief, which LT struggled through. No one else had much to say after him. I offered to pray with anyone that wanted to and then we turned to for the rest of the afternoon. That evening, me and several of the Marines huddled up for a Bible study and prayer. We talked about the gospel and the eternal assurance that Jesus offers all of us. We prayed together and recommitted ourselves to God and to our purpose for being out there. When the day was over and I laid my head down on my stiff Zondervan study Bible, which had been my only pillow since the beginning of the deployment, I stared up into the starry night sky like any other night and reflected on the day. If it had been me earlier that day, or the day prior, or any day ahead, what would my legacy be? Had I lived my life to its fullest measure? Would I eventually make it home and be afforded another chance to? What a day. What a terrible day. I was angry and deeply saddened. We all were.

BATTLEFIELD INVESTIGATION

We were ordered down to FOB Jackson to debrief with Command as well as spend time with investigators to dissect the events of April 6 and determine what exactly went wrong. When we pulled up through the FOB entry point, all the Alpha Company Marines who were not on post were lined up along the road in solidarity. We pulled in, parked, and offloaded all our gear. Major Wood huddled us up to give his thoughts. He told us about a brief memorial ceremony that took place at Camp Leatherneck, the last stop before Smith and Rast's bodies were sent home. By divine intervention it seemed, our 3rd Squad just happened to be at Leatherneck for a resupply during that time and were able to pay their respects before the bodies were flown back to the States. Major Wood told us he had already talked to the drone pilot who fired the shot and that the pilot asserted he would put a bullet in his own head instantly if it would bring back our Marines. Among other things Major Wood told us, 'Boys, in no other life circumstance is this good advice but you have to bottle this up, all of the emotion, and deal with it later because you are headed right back out on mission and still have a long road ahead. The eyes of the Battalion are on you, and you are kicking ass. Don't let up now.' He told us we were highlighted and respected across the Battalion and that despite this occurrence we were making waves in our operational arena. He said, 'I am going to read something to you boys, and I want you to listen to every word.' Then he recited a powerful quote I had never heard before:

> *It is not the critic who counts; not the man who points out how the strong man stumbles, or where the doer of deeds could have done them better. The credit belongs to the man who is actually in the arena, whose face is marred by dust and sweat and blood; who strives valiantly, who errs, who comes short again and again; who spends himself in a worthy cause; who at the best knows in the end the triumph of high achievement, and who at the worst, if he fails, at least fails while daring greatly, so that his place shall never be with those cold and timid souls who neither know victory nor defeat.'*
>
> Theodore Roosevelt

Wood said, 'In the days ahead don't let anyone's judgement affect you men. You are men in the arena and you're doing a damn good job.'

After Major Wood, Gunny Coleman shared with us some of his many deployment losses. He said, 'Gents it's sad, but it is what it is. You just have to pick up and carry on. We are Marines, and this is the life we chose.' He was right. This is the life we chose; the life

I chose, and I did so knowing the risks. I was among my own band of brothers fighting on behalf of ideals that are worth the sacrifice and we were successfully pounding back the tyrannical control of a brutally oppressive enemy force. Someone once said, 'People sleep peaceably in their beds at night only because rough men stand ready to do violence on their behalf.' I was one of those rough men. I was the man in the arena. When Gunny Coleman finished, I felt a heightened sense of confidence and brash boldness to fight on. We all did.

We settled in for the night and for the first time perhaps in the deployment thus far I contemplated how potentially impactful our efforts actually were toward the grand mission in Afghanistan. We were a very small part of a big force in a dynamic battlespace but were fully engaged in the Battle for Sangin and we were making a difference. I bowed my head before God and thanked Him for letting me be a part of it all and went to sleep.

The next day we were visited by our Battalion Commander and Battalion Sergeant Major, both voicing their condolences and respect for how we were handling the mission we had been tasked with. Then they made introductions to the investigation team, and we began deliberations. We all sat individually with investigators and were asked questions that collectively painted the picture of the sequence of events that led up to Smith and Rast being killed. Unknown to me at the time, this was the first ever friendly fire incident involving a Predator drone. How this would be viewed in the long run was out of our control. The fact remained that we were caught in a complex enemy engagement and regardless of who would be decidedly at fault, there were any number of other bad outcomes that could have transpired. We were all in different positions on the battlefield and our recollection from numerous vantage points would vary some but from mine, I did not recall any dereliction of duty. Combat is chaotic and there is no single method of decision-making that always results in the preservation of life. 'Control the chaos' is the tag line for unit leadership during combat but that 'control' is elusive. Even when the right combat tactics are deployed and all contingencies are set in place, everything can so rapidly change. It's just war and in war people die.

A major storm system began to blow in late in the day. Word came down in the mid-afternoon of a credible threat against FOB Jackson that night. The enemy was apparently coordinating an effort to overrun the entire FOB in the middle of the night amidst the storms, given we would have no air support. Bold plan if it was real. There was no way they would be able to successfully overthrow us though. Even if they managed to breach our perimeter we would inflict such an incredibly severe response on them within our walls that they would retreat or surrender. The whole FOB got amped up on high alert. FOB Jackson was not very big, and it was right on the edge of Sangin's most urban area, making for easily concealable movement of large enemy forces right up to the perimeter on most sides. The units at Jackson locked down the base, beefed up perimeter security and all entries, put snipers up on the roof of the highest buildings in the FOB for overwatch and set up mortar positions for indirect fire along the perimeters. Given Jackson was not our home station and perimeter security was sufficient without us, we positioned our trucks for a quick start up and movement to the perimeter for support with our turret heavy weapons, prepped our personal gear for night battle, established our general reaction plan should we be awoken to an attack and then turned in for the night to try to get some sleep. Like many other nights, I laid down with my TOPS fixed-blade firmly grasped in my right hand and my rifle laying in my cot beside me with a mag inserted. As I started to fall asleep, I recited Psalm 4:8 to myself as I had done almost every night prior, 'I will lie down and sleep in peace, for you alone Lord make me dwell in safety.' Hours later I woke up to the morning sunrise. The attack never materialized, and we carried on about our day.

We had been 'dark' on communications home since April 6, which is standard when Marines are killed as an assurance that the families back home would receive the news through the proper channels rather than by word spreading from us overseas. The ban was lifted on our last day at Jackson on April 9, which meant both families had been sufficiently notified. While loaded with fresh supplies and soon to make the drive back to Alcatraz, I decided to call my dad to tell him what happened myself. We were a Texas Marine unit, and it was only a matter of time before Smith and Rast's deaths were broadcast on the evening news for my parents to see. I hadn't spoken with either of them in a couple weeks and should they see the news without hearing from me first, who knows what they might think. I went to the phone center, which happened to be empty, and dialed my dad's phone number, each key stroke more reluctantly than the last. I had been angry, bitter, and remorseful by all of this in the few preceding days but had not shed a tear yet for some reason. The moment my dad answered the phone it all came out. Something about talking to my father brought tears I couldn't control and I could hardly say anything at all. He remained silent and I just sobbed and sobbed. After a few moments I muttered it out, 'Smith's dead. Smith and Doc Rast are dead.' The hardened Marine came off and the wounded little boy inside of me was laid bare before my father for the first time in a long time. The sobbing continued. I eventually pulled myself together and told him that they were killed in a battle that I was also engaged in and that I was sure he would see it on the news in the next few days. He thanked me for telling him and told me he would figure out the right way to inform the rest of the family. I assured him I was alright and told him I loved him, which he reciprocated. Neither of us knew much of what to say after.

As expected, in the following days their deaths were all over the news. I can't imagine how my mom felt. She was coincidentally Smith's college advisor for a time and admired him. She was comforted leading into the deployment knowing that he was one of my unit leaders given the breadth of his previous wartime experience. Now her assurance had turned into amplified worry. If Smith, being as experienced as he was, could be killed, what were my chances as a Marine on my first deployment? How does a loving mother cope with such stress? How did Smith and Rast's mothers and the thousands of others that received the final news of their own sons and daughters' deaths during the war? It was all so bitterly tragic and still is.

We made it back to Alcatraz unscathed and found that the recent storms had destroyed our meager little encampment. Our belongings were scattered across our corner of the compound. Everything was wet and covered in mud. We sorted things out, straightened everything up and began preparing for our next operation. We were heading back out on mission the next day. In many ways I was emboldened by the recent events. We sustained a heavy blow but were resiliently getting right back in the fight. Honestly, I was surprised we had only just sustained casualties. 3/5 had ten KIAs and thirty-five wounded in action in their first three days of operations.[13] 2nd Recon took their first death by IED in the first few days they took over PB Alcatraz. Of course, both of those units were early movers in trailblazing the valley but still, it was surprising that we had made it as long as we did without any ourselves. We started mission briefing and Huff recited all the fresh intel that he got while at Jackson, which included notice of more fresh new enemy arrivals from foreign countries. It didn't matter to us. Whoever got in our way was going to pay for it, and especially now.

---

13. Bing West, *One Million Steps: A Marine Platoon at War* (New York: Random House, 2014), p.23.

Chapter 8

CHANGING TIDES

'For everything there is a season, and a time for every matter under heaven.'

Ecclesiastes 3:1

We were back in full-scale operation for the weeks following April 6 and were pushing a fast pace again. We found out that some of our 3rd Squad Marines in Delaram suffered a big IED strike the same night we arrived back at Alcatraz. They had responded to a call from the Georgian Military for help at night and hit an 80lb pressure plate that exploded underneath the front end of the MATV they were driving, obliterating the attached mine roller, both of the truck's front tires, the front end and the radiator. The guys in the truck sustained TBIs (Traumatic Brain Injuries) and hearing loss. All survived the blast without life-threatening injury, thankfully. This made five IED strikes on 2nd Platoon, six if you include the blasting cap and failed explosion that hit our 6x6 on April 6.

There were big Marine Corps command shifts happening in the Sangin valley over the month of April and we found ourselves at the mercy of it all. 1st Battalion, 5th Marines arrived to replace 3/5 and started taking over. 2nd Recon began scaling back in preparation for their departure as well. With these transitions came changes in operational dynamics. As the change of command processes developed, the overarching mission focuses and supporting strategies came under review and timely adaptations were made. 3/5 and 2nd Recon's operational tempos slowed down. It happened too often in Afghanistan and Iraq that Marines were killed with only days left in their deployments after having survived the preceding months of combat. This was perfectly exampled on my first patrol outside the wire when the 3/25 turret gunner nearly took rounds to the head days before he was heading home. It seemed that the overarching mentality of the departing units was to pull back just enough to establish a strong defensive front and de-escalate the engagements to a minimum until the other units fully took over. This put a lot of heat on Route 611 as a line of demarcation with less intentional foot patrolling in the green zone each day, which resulted in increased demand for our gun truck presence on the road around the clock again. Our QRF element received repeated calls day and night to provide presence and security on the 611 as new Battalion and Regimental Commanders came in and out to survey the valley. There was an uptick in roadside IEDs given the diminished foot patrol presence in the valley. We found ourselves performing controlled detonations with EOD teams in tow near daily, it felt like.

We were also constantly on mounted and dismounted observation patrols based on hot intel and new Commanders' intents as they test drove their new commands and learned the Sangin operational arena. We interlaced foot patrols and sniper missions in between mounted missions. Our more creative high-risk patrol plans started to be met with added resistance. The units going home didn't want to get pulled into aiding us out of any unnecessarily bad situations and the new units were still learning what muscles to flex. Our own foot patrols lowered in frequency as a result, with added green zone entry limitations. Our sniper patrols focused on positioning for distance observation and surprise disruption of enemy activity from planned locations along the 611. We also shook up our typical flow of patrol functions and spread out role responsibilities depending on the day's missions and the teams put together to tackle them. The majority of our resupplies during that time were trips in the middle of the night to Nolay, given most days were filled with various mission orders. This put sleep deprivation stress back on us heavy.

While on the road, MAMs were ever present, watching us closely everywhere we went, all the time and in higher volume than before. On one occasion we made a short stop to solicit a chat with a local leader and I noticed a MAM discreetly taking pictures of us under his clothing. I barreled out my truck at him, patted him down and looked through his phone, which had a multitude of photos of our trucks and intentionally zoomed in shots of our faces. I wrenched flexi cuffs on his wrists, put a blacked-out bag over his head and loaded him into the truck. Our procedure for arrests was to drop off detainees at the nearest FOB, where investigative elements took custody of them and vetted them out. If he was clean, they would bring him right back to where he was arrested with a fresh meal and bottle of water. If not, they would ship him off to any number of destinations in or out of the country for interrogations and long-term detainment. We notified FOB Inkerman that we had a detainee to drop off and Marines were waiting at the ECP to take custody of him when we arrived.

THE NEWS WE FEARED

In late spring, as 1/5 began to find their operational flow in southern Sangin, the hellacious battle ground that many had fought so fiercely to secure, the valley reignited. Air-to-ground ordnance drops, IED explosions and firefights all returned en masse. We hoped this would mean the continuation of our involvement in Sangin long term, but regional command had other plans. By the end of April, we received the news we all feared. I did not want to believe it would happen, but word came down that our time in Sangin was coming to an end.

1/5 had enough fresh manpower within their battalion to take over the region entirely and our efforts were needed elsewhere. Despite our lobbying to remain in the fight in Sangin, orders came down that we would be heading to Delaram to pick up our Drug Interdiction Mission along the Iranian border, which had been initially postponed.

It was a transitional period in the valley like one chapter ending and another beginning. 3/5 was gone, 2nd Recon was weeks away from leaving for home also and 1/5 was in full force. PB Alcatraz was scheduled to become an established FOB and Combat Engineering units were soon to make the trek north to begin building an actual base out of our minimally fortified mud-wall compounds. The Marine Corps was still progressively advancing control and stability throughout Sangin and our enemy's foothold was weakening day by day, despite their seemingly never-ending inflow of foreign reinforcements. It felt like our time there in operations was getting cut short. We had contributed faithfully in battle and blood to regional stabilization and advancement of the broader mission of the Battle for Sangin. Two months of constant contact with enemy forces, countless hours of around the clock sleepless missions, multiple IED strikes, numerous repelled ambush attacks involving enemy snipers, heavy machine guns, RPGs and mortars, more close calls than any of us could put together, numerous enemy dead including unit commanders, and two of our own KIA. It had been a wild ride. When it was all said and done, the Battle for Sangin was recognized as the bloodiest battle campaign in the entire twenty-year war in Afghanistan. In that time, we were told Sangin had been dubbed the 'deadliest place on earth', which was uncanny to hear given we contributed directly to that title and on both sides of the fighting. It felt like our deployment was coming to an end, but we weren't even halfway through it yet. While bittersweet in the worst way and unable to turn the tide, we reset our focus on our new mission.

Our date of departure was set to be May 3 and we weren't getting out of it. The harvest was just beginning in the green zone. For the previous month the fields had been covered in beautiful white, pink and red poppy flowers. By the end of April, the locals were starting to strip the flower petals and leave the bulbs to dry out, which they would eventually harvest and sell to the Taliban, who would attempt to export them to Iran and Pakistan for heroin production and distribution. In effect, we started our deployment during the early opium production season in Sangin, one of the last major production regions of its kind, and we would now move to intercept the same crop on its way out of the country as our enemy attempted to export it for profit.

We spent our final days at Alcatraz breaking down and packing up our meager encampment around missions. The mood was both serene from our accomplishments and dismal from both our mandated departure and the feeling that we could still do more. In the early dark morning of May 2 we geared up and loaded into our trucks for the last time at PB Alcatraz. Receiving the green light for departure from the Recon COC, we made our way down the narrow entry drive to Route 611, chunked up the duce to the meager ANP (Afghan National Policy) security post situated roadside, and pushed south, never to return. So much had happened in so little time and before we knew it, we were gone. The drive south past Inkerman, through the bazaar and past Jackson was difficult for me. I felt like we were leaving the fight, and I very adamantly did not want to go. I was emotionally invested in a deep way and was right where I wanted to be. I was at the tip of the spear in the most contested and kinetic area of operation in the war at that time. It was everything I joined for, trained for, and sacrificed so much to be a part of but orders are orders. We stopped at Nolay for a day, and then on May 3 we left Sangin for good.

REST AND RECOVERY

We made a pitstop at Camp Leatherneck to rest and regear for a few days before Delaram. Our trucks were gasping for maintenance, some of our gear was beyond recovery and we were all more strung out than we realized. A few hours after leaving Sangin we arrived at Leatherneck's ECP (Entry Choke Point) just as the sun began to rise. We pulled in and parked in an open staging area not far from one of the main chow halls. It didn't take long to recognize how wildly filthy and rag tag we were compared to everyone else who at Leatherneck could shower and wash clothes regularly and had access to all forms of hygiene amenities. Sleep deprivation, hygienic neglect, sparce eating habits and extreme levels of physical and emotional stress were all on full display.

We made our way to the chow hall, and I got a ton of looks; every one of them creating more internal tension in me than the last. I remember being wound up so tight, ready to twist off at whoever dared confront me about my appearance. We were so far out of regulation, but could any reasonable person expect anything different? When I approached the entrance into the air-conditioned chow hall there was a First Sergeant (2nd highest enlisted rank in the Corps) ripping into a couple of junior Marines in the chow line ahead of me for not moving fast enough in their selections. I thought, 'Here we go. Let's see what he makes of me ...' To my surprise, the moment his eyes caught mine he looked me up and down and his demeanor immediately softened. He approached me, grabbed me by the shoulder and said with a soft voice, 'Come up here warrior. You get up to the front of the line and you take as long as you want to Corporal.' I was completely taken back and began to get choked up. I fully expected to be publicly shamed and ripped into for my filthy appearance, which would very much be in keeping with the normal way of things in the Corps, but instead I was shown distinction and a warrior's respect. I don't know if I've ever felt more honored in my entire life. Everyone in eyeshot watched the gesture, cleared a path in mutual agreement, quieted down and ushered me forward in recognition of the outward toll that the war had already taken on me. I walked through the chow line like a hero among heroes and sat down to eat what seemed at the time to be the most delicious food my taste buds had ever experienced. Everything was comforting, I could have as much of anything I wanted without restriction, and I was under no rigid time constraint. It all felt so refreshingly normal and so amazing.

We spent the next few days at Leatherneck to rest and recoup while maintenance was being done on our trucks and other gear; and professionally at that rather than by our novice jerry-rigging for the first time in a long time. We got settled in and took advantage of the opportunity to clean up. It had been weeks since we last showered or washed clothes. Ironically, the dirtiest I felt on the entire deployment was always in the few hours immediately after scrubbing off all the baked-in dirt and grime. Just like a pig enjoys their swallow, it was often more comfortable to just stay dirty.

We enjoyed the chance to let loose for a little while with very few agenda demands. It was truly R&R and I spent as much time as I could resting. One evening while at Leatherneck a few of us went to one of the smaller chow halls for dinner. We sat down with our food, and I looked up in shock at one of the small TVs that was playing the news. The announcement was made that Osama bin Laden had finally been found and killed. I had a hard time accepting it. It felt so unreal that I actually thought it might be a fabricated political stunt. This meant that we reached the just end to what had been a decades-long pursuit of the most notorious global terrorist of our lifetime. I strangely struggled to feel a sense of celebration by it though. It meant that our battlefield opponents would try to hit us even harder in retaliation in the days following. In fact, we found out that just a couple days after we left PB Alcatraz, enemy forces in Sangin launched a large-scale attack on the PB, resulting in numerous friendly casualties. Among other things, they hit the Marines there with new Iranian RPGs that were able to explode overhead without a direct impact, meaning they could rain down shrapnel on the Marines behind the PB mud walls. It was said to be one hell of a fight and we were very upset that we weren't there to be a part of it. This was an uncommon attack and likely in response to bin Laden's death. Regardless of the heightened threat levels, our finding and killing bin Laden was an enormously defining moment in the war that I was still fully engaged in.

Well rested and tuned up, on the morning of May 10 around 0400 we loaded up and pushed to FOB Delaram ready to hit it hard again. The base was big compared to those in Sangin but very empty. It housed the closest large airstrip to Iran in Southern Afghanistan and was strategically important given tensions with Iran were high at the time. The FOB was on somewhat of a hillside that overlooked the Khash River basin and the town district beyond it. There was a sizable ANA Base (Afghan National Army) on the other side of the river and numerous small outposts in the region, including a couple manned by smaller Marine detachments. The region was riddled with evidence of the Soviet–Afghan war. There were two blown up and ransacked Russian tanks along the roadside in different places that had undoubtedly been sitting in the exact same location since they were first immobilized in the Soviet–Afghan war thirty years prior. Live Soviet ordnance was unearthed regularly all around Delaram as well as other pieces of random Soviet military equipment too big for the local Afghans to move around and salvage. Delaram had some agricultural green fields but was predominantly a desert-scape that more resembled Twentynine Palms, California, with lifeless rocky mountains and desert plains extending in every direction. The townships were all the same-style mud hut and cinderblock buildings we had seen elsewhere and the only paved road was the main interstate. It was mostly rural with pockets of dense population and generally rough.

When we pulled into the base, 3rd Squad was there to greet us and it was great to see them. They helped us offload everything from the trucks and took us to our new digs. Once unpacked, Major Wood brought 2nd Platoon into the Alpha Company Command Post, welcomed us to Delaram, and issued our orders. The opium harvest was still under way across southern Afghanistan, and the drug exports weren't in high volume just yet. Ahead of the flow of opium exports, we were to begin mounted patrols for the remainder of May while reassuming a regional role as the twenty-four-hour gun truck Quick Reaction Force. We would pick up any missions outside the wire, reinforcement support or otherwise, within 60+ miles of the FOB. The Drug Interdiction Mission along the Iranian border would pick up steam sometime in mid-June. With plenty of work to do and hopefully plenty of action to come with it, we hit the ground running once again.

BACK IN THE SADDLE AGAIN

Missions started immediately. We organized our new operational structure between our three squads in coordination with other regional units and established SOPs (Standard Operating Procedures) for our new operations. Over the next month we traveled all over the place. Regional stability was spotty. There were plenty of ANA (Afghan National Army), ANP (Afghan National Police) and AHP (Afghan Highway Patrol) in the region, but outside of the Delaram township everything was very spread out and a lot of the friendly outposts were isolated. AHP outposts along the highways were regularly overrun by enemy forces in the middle of the night and our friendly forces who manned them were captured and tortured to death. On one occasion over the course of a two-week period civilians brought us more than fifteen decapitated and mutilated bodies they had found of AHP/ANP personnel that the enemy had captured and brutally murdered. The enemy forces would either leave the bodies at the torture site for the civilians to find or place them strategically through the township or rural area with the intent of inflicting fear and coercion. They were ruthless and cruel. Civilian collateral damage was not infrequent either. There were massive roadside IEDs all along the major highways and civilians hit them a lot. One of the biggest civilian catastrophes during that time in the region involved a packed civilian bus that was ripped apart by a huge IED intended for us. It killed or injured almost thirty civilians on board, women, children, and even babies included. The

Taliban didn't care at all. They were willing to do anything to advance their tyrannical jihad and they self-justified any action of cruelty, even on the innocent, if it furthered their goals for power and control.

In certain places, pressure plates were as bad or worse in volume as in Sangin. Just prior to our arrival, a Georgian Army patrol in Delaram had suffered eleven casualties from numerous pressure plates hits and a follow-on ambush. It started when one of their guys stepped on an IED that blew his legs off. Another soldier came to aide him and stepped on an IED also. Then a third did the same thing and while the rest of their unit experienced the pandemonium of trying to save the three critically wounded soldiers, the enemy ambushed them with small arms fire and mortars. Many of the casualties didn't survive.

Another major threat that we were warned about was enemy IDF (indirect fire, or artillery mortars). This was a frequent attack method in the region given they could strike accurately from more than two clicks away (1 click = 1,000 meters). Let's not forget about the RPGs either. We had plenty of close calls with rocket propelled grenades in Sangin obviously, but I always doubted they could actually penetrate our trucks. Boy was I ever wrong. When we got to Delaram a couple of our guys were detached to join a mission in Musa Qala, which was just north of Sangin. Within days of their arrival a Georgian Army truck patrol came under attack and one of the trucks received an RPG direct hit. The rocket-propelled grenade penetrated the front windshield of their MRAP and detonated inside the cab literally on the Vehicle Commander (front passenger), which obliterated his body, and the concussion and shrapnel of the explosion inside the truck's hull killed all five of the other soldiers inside. The explosion was so powerful that it lodged bone fragments of the Vehicle Commander's exploded skull into the metal plating of the front passenger door. Our guys sent us pictures of the aftermath, proving without a doubt that RPGs were to be taken seriously, even in our armored vehicles.

We made internal adjustments in our mission methodology to account for our new environment. It was the same cat and mouse game, but on a different playing field with new rules. Our patrols proved to be less combat oriented and more investigative. IED discoveries were reported regularly from various sources, and we would locate and dispose of them with our regimental EOD teams in tow. For a time, it seemed like we were control detonating a new roadside IED every single day. Most of the time EOD's C4 would cut through the IEDs, disabling them enough to be dismantled, but other times the ammonium nitrate would ignite with the C4 and make for huge concussive explosions that would send shockwaves rolling across the desert floor like supercharged wakes on a body of water. When we weren't investigating IEDs, we were tasked with any number of one-off minor missions like taking supplies to some of the further friendly outposts, escorting VIPs from one friendly installment to another, transporting sensitive items to and from Camp Leatherneck, etc.

The QRF missions came less frequently than in Sangin, but they were more diverse. On one occasion, we received mission orders to prepare to reinforce a night raid in the area via helo insert. We collected extra ammo and grenades, prepped night battle gear, shed all other nonessentials, stocked up on extra flex cuffs and blackout hoods for any prisoner captures, and staged right by the FOB helo pad for a quick pick up. A British Task Force had good intel on a high-value target that they were going to hit in the middle of the night. If they happened to encounter heavy resistance, we would immediately hop on two pre-staged choppers and sprint in to help beat down the opposition. We weren't told anything beyond that. If called up, they would brief us in the air. To our disappointment the raid was a British success without needing our involvement and we were told to stand down sometime after midnight. The next morning, we were right back out on mission tasks anyway.

A couple of days after the raid, late one evening we received a call for immediate QRF. A small MARSOC (Marine Special Operations Command) unit hit a huge IED on their way to Delaram. We bolted to their position and were surprised to find there were only two MATVs in their convoy. Not only that, but there were only four Marines total, two in each truck, which was unusually thin. The truck that took the hit was upside down and located at the front of a 50m-long slide streak in the pavement, meaning they were really moving fast. It was crazy that the two Marines who took the hit were still alive and even more so that neither were even really injured. They were lucky. We pushed off the road 100m or so in every direction and set up a 360° security until wreckers showed up a couple of hours later to pick up the busted truck.

Days after helping MARSOC, we received a QRF 'Critical Recovery Mission'. A Scan Eagle UAV (Unmanned Aerial Vehicle) went down eight and a half clicks south of Delaram in the middle of the sand dune desert and we were tasked to either retrieve it before the enemy got their hands on it or take it back if they beat us to it. We pushed out in the dark at 0030 (am) into an area of the desert where no Marines had ever been before. There were no roads, NVGs were low performing given the moon was not full and we were blacked out, using no lights. We were warned to expect ambushes, booby traps and possible IDF, and the longer we waited to get out there the greater those risks became. Two clicks outside of Delaram the rough terrain turned into tall hills and deep wadis with very soft sands. Our lead truck got stuck several times and I ended up in the driver's seat getting it unstuck each time by deflating the tires and aggressively rocking the heavy steel ship forward and reverse until I nudged it out of the sand ruts it bogged down in.

After several hours we found the crash-landed UAV and approached it carefully. The drivers were doing 360° scans with their IR screens to see if anyone was watching. Even through NVGs it was pretty clear that there were no footprints or tracks of any kind and the UAV appeared untouched. We inspected it for booby traps anyway and once deemed safe we loaded it up and headed back. After the lead truck driver got stuck for the fourth time I permanently took over and drove all the way back to Delaram.

We pulled up to the backside of the FOB just as the sun breached the horizon the next morning. We had less than an hour to change clothes, clean up and get to the funeral ceremony that Alpha Company was finally putting on for Rast and Smith now that we were all in one place. Near the end of the ceremony, Lt Huff took the podium. Up to that point I don't think he spoke to any of us at length about the events of April 6 after it happened, so I was very interested to hear what he had to say. The battlefield investigation we all took part in had previously concluded the incident was a result of the fog of war. Some of the guys disagreed adamantly with that conclusion. I thought it was a fair determination at the time. I felt able to reconcile the whole thing given my understanding of the circumstances. Huff was a different story though. He was the unit commander on the ground, regardless of fault. I'm sure he carried more guilt than he let any of us see, whether warranted or not. I would have. I listened to his speech intently, reflecting on each word and later journaled about it:

'LT was not particularly grandiose. He did not say much and what he did have to say was softly spoken and shrouded with quietly controlled emotion. He spoke of the highest stature that Smith had in the platoon and the infectious personality that Rast captured us all into. He quoted from Smith's war journal, reciting what are now famous words among our platoon, "Sometimes you find yourself in the middle of nowhere. Sometimes in the middle of nowhere you find yourself." We've all found out what we are made of out here. The full toll of the physical and emotional stress is not easy to describe but the pressure has revealed things about each of us that few other life situations would. I am proud of having gone through what we have and to still be in the fight. On the other hand, I'm not sure these experiences will result well in the long run for all of us. Time will tell for me and the boys, but not for Smith and Rast. Their legacies in this life are now set, but what an honorable end they achieved in laying down their lives for the benefit of others. I will never forget that.'

AFGHAN HIGHWAY PATROL COMPOUND

Another few days went by, and we 2nd Squad convoyed to one of the bigger AHP (Afghan Highway Patrol) compounds a few clicks away from FOB Delaram. One other Alpha Company squad and one of our sniper teams was posted there alongside the Afghanis. This compound was to Delaram what Alcatraz was to Jackson or Nolay, a small, minimally fortified outpost located far enough away from the FOB that those on it would be up a creek if heavily attacked. We pulled in before dusk. The Marines were strolling around in shorts and flip-flops with no one breathing down their necks about regulations, which was refreshing. We parked, took our gear off and joined some Marines on the steps of a small building in the center of the compound. They had a laptop situated on a small table in the open courtyard area adjacent to the steps with a movie playing. We joked around, laughed and enjoyed the opportunity to mentally check out for a little while watching a movie.

Several minutes went by and out of nowhere, BOOM!!! A massive blast exploded right on the other side of the compound wall no more than 60m away from where we sat. Freaking enemy IDF, and they were dialed in too. The blast hit, there was a second of complete silence and surprise and then, as if on a straight line in a track meet when the pistol fired, everyone instantaneously jumped up and took off sprinting in all directions for cover in avoidance of the next incoming round. 2nd Squad sprinted back to our trucks and threw on gear as quickly as we could, preparing to storm out of the compound and chase down whoever fired at us. Our gunners were in turrets prepping heavy weapons as we fired up the trucks, hastily performed radio checks and got ready to push. ISR (overwatch drone) was called in and we were moving out as fast as possible, all under the angst of knowing the next mortar might land right on top of us. Just as we started to pull off toward the AHP exit to hunt down our attackers, a Marine with a radio in hand and no gear on jogged up to my truck waiving us down while laughing. This was unexpected. He said, 'False alarm false alarm! It was the ANA (Afghan National Army) screwing around with grenades.' Unbelievable! We all began to laugh and let our guards down. What had just been a calm and careless moment together instantly turned into a life-or-death attack (so we thought), but then it reverted right back. We took our gear off and made our way back to the movie. The entire outpost thought we were getting shelled, except for the few ANA idiots that carelessly lobbed the grenade.

The best part of the whole story though was not our wasted 'life or death' response or the ANA's ideocracy of playing with grenades inside a compound. The best part was when we walked back to the steps that we had congregated on prior to the explosion, we noticed the movie was paused. Surprised and confused, we began to question, 'Who took the time to pause the movie while we thought we were under attack?' The laptop was sitting in the middle of the wide-open courtyard behind no cover whatsoever. Up walks Sgt Ashley, who quickly conceded, 'Oh yeah, I paused the movie for us, guys. You're all welcome.' Infectious laughter broke out among all of us. When the danger-close explosion hit, everyone's first reaction was to sprint for cover in fear of getting hit by the next incoming enemy mortar, but not Ashley. His first instinctual reaction was to run straight to the laptop to pause the movie so we would not lose our place for after the attack, and THEN sprint for cover to save his life. Ha ha ha! It was hysterical and this was a classic Ashley move.

Chapter 9

CONTROL THE CHAOS

'We don't rise to the level of our expectations; we fall to the level of our training.'

Archilochus

It was early evening on May 28, 2011. My squad was on duty as standby QRF when the call came in. The initial radio transmission was, 'IED DIRECT HIT. MARINES TRAPPED UNDER BURNING MRAP, REQUESTING QRF & AIR SUPPORT IMMEDIATELY!'

I was laid back with my feet kicked up in my driver's seat reading a book when Peck burst out of the CP (Command Post) more frantic than I had ever seen him. He said, 'Get the guys and mount up we have to go now!' I said, 'Wait, what happened?' Peck replied, 'It's 3rd Squad; they got hit bad and they're trapped in a burning truck, we have to go now.' I snapped-to quick, ran to get the rest of the guys and we sprinted back to the trucks geared up and headed out as fast as we could. 3rd Squad was over twenty-two clicks west of Delaram, which is a very long drive outside the wire for an emergency, and they were also far away from any main roads. Using less caution than normal, we pushed as fast as we could against the rugged terrain. Once we got through Delaram's City District Center, we could see the black smoke cylinder high in the sky coming from the inflamed truck far out on the horizon. The further we drove, the further their location seemed to be. We were all frantic to get a good understanding of what we were heading into, but radio communication was spotty. The guys on the ground were tied up with the COC and medevac helos coordinating the pickup and we were left in the dark. After all we had experienced in Sangin, our minds were on the follow-on ambush. We were well prepared to address that. What I was most nervous about though was handling the carnage inside that truck. God forbid any of my friends burn alive trapped inside the steel hull of that MRAP. Just a few minutes after passing through the Delaram urban center we got off the main asphalt highway and began traversing crop fields. It was not the fastest option and some of the terrain we could only crawl across. Given all we knew about the region and how the enemy operated, though, we were very cautious to not take the easiest/quickest route. It was likely enough that the enemy would anticipate the call for help and a QRF unit being dispatched from Delaram to render aid. If the enemy awareness and motivation was high enough it wouldn't take them long to get another hasty IED in the ground along an anticipated avenue of approach and we would all be double screwed if we took an IED strike on the way to helping 3rd Squad.

A few details finally began to make it through while we were enroute. The truck that took the hit was Cpl Cline's MRAP, which had four Marines and a Corpsman on board, along with seven hundred-plus high-explosive grenades for the Mk19, several LAW rockets, and a healthy amount of other munitions. The IED flipped the MRAP completely upside down and set it ablaze. We all knew what that meant. The turret gunner was dead for sure and given the size of the explosion it was very likely that the others were also. The black smoke billowing up in the sky got larger and thicker. We panicked and were going as fast as we could, but it wasn't fast enough. Finally, two medevac helos appeared from the north and closed in on 3rd Squad's position. The terrain was flat enough that we could see one helo descending toward the smoke tower while the accompanying gunship circled the blast site overhead to provide aerial cover. It only took them a few minutes before the helo on the ground dusted off and both Blackhawks gained altitude and flew right toward and past us heading east to the shock trauma center at FOB Delaram, where the rest of our Corpsman staff were waiting to receive the casualties.

The pickup seemed quick. I didn't know if that was a good sign or bad. Maybe they were so quick because the other guys got all the trapped Marines out. Maybe some of the trapped Marines were still trapped but already dead so the helos were rushing the guys out that still had a chance. Maybe they're all dead and that helicopter was filled with five body bags of mangled flesh. It felt just like the moment after Smith and Rast were hit when the call came through our radios pronouncing one Marine as 'critical' and one 'routine'. Uncertainty meant anxiety and we waited helplessly to be told who made it out and who didn't. When the helos cleared the area, we finally made direct contact with 3rd Squad. Not too long after that we arrived at their position. The three remaining trucks were fanned out posting security while the truck that took the strike sat ablaze in the middle of them laying belly up. It was significantly damaged and the HE grenades and other miscellaneous rounds were still cooking off inside the flames. Numerous major components had been blown off and more than half of the exterior steel on one side was charred black amidst the continuing flames. We broadened the 360° security, filling in their gaps, and then got the full scoop on what all took place.

At the time of the explosion, 3rd Squad was headed back to FOB Delaram on patrol. They had already discovered and neutralized another IED previously on their patrol and just ahead of this strike everything was relatively calm. In as unexpected a fashion as any IED strike, a massive explosion rang out and the guys watched the targeted MRAP, which was Truck 2 in the patrol, lift up in the air in a cloud of fire and dust and land on its top. The IED exploded under the rear axle, flipping the 35,000lb vehicle back over front and setting it on fire. The turret was crushed in and buried. Marines in the other three trucks quickly set up security to prepare for any follow-on ambush and then carefully approached the burning MRAP to assess the carnage. Cpl Walker dismounted and cautiously made his way toward the truck, very cognizant of the likelihood of there being accompanying pressure plates in the immediate vicinity. While he approached, the other Marines were in communication with the COC spinning up QRF. Cpl Cline, who was in the front passenger seat, eventually stumbled out of the smoke filled truck through his passenger door almost completely delirious. When the explosion struck, Cline was knocked unconscious and whether it was from the concussion of the initial blast, slamming his head against the interior thick metal wall of the vehicle, or both, he suffered a severe stage three concussion, on top of tears in his shoulder, severe nerve damage down one arm, and bad smoke inhalation causing permanent damage to his lungs. Cpl Dimas, who was in the driver's seat, came out behind Cline with blood flowing down half of his face. He fell out of the truck and when he stood up he racked a round into the chamber of his rifle, blurted out some unintelligible expletives and was looking for the enemy to shoot. Walker quickly calmed him and sat him down a safe distance away. He had also been knocked out cold, suffered a TBI with an accompanying brain bleed, had a gash across his head that required five staples, and suffered spine compression, a broken collar bone and a broken leg.

When Cline and Dimas initially awoke after getting knocked out from the explosion, they yelled back to check on the other Marines. Seeing flames begin to build, Dimas frantically reached around for a fire extinguisher and found one but couldn't get it to operate. Dimas and Cline began shoving and kicking their doors in the upside-down combat vehicle, which were lodged shut, to try to get them open in fear of burning to death. Doc Lewallen, who also miraculously survived the explosion, was in the back of the truck fighting to get the rear hatch doors to open while Apgar remained completely unconscious and questionably alive. No one had any confidence at that point that Vega, who was in the turret, could possibly have survived. While they were yelling back and forth at each other, there was no sign of life from Vega. The little that they could see of his legs were lifeless and the rest of his body appeared to be crushed and buried between the turret opening and the ground. Smoke and flames were quickly starting to engulf everything inside, obscuring all the Marines' ability to assess the others' situations, let alone breathe as the smoke entrapped them.

Lewallen eventually gave up on the rear doors and found the escape hatch that resided in the ceiling near the rear of the truck. He unlatched it, then kicked it aggressively over and over until it dislodged. He then snaked Apgar's now partially conscious body through the small opening to Walker, who was able to drag Apgar out the other side. When Apgar exited the vehicle, he started to come to a little bit and, though completely dazed, he grabbed a rifle and went to post security behind one of the other trucks in anticipation of an ambush. Walker then went to pull Lewallen out, who at that point began to feel the excruciating pain of having had both feet crushed in the truck's tumble. Lewallen's concussion delirium and adrenaline had temporarily masked his pain while he was unknowingly ramming his severely injured feet into the escape hatch, thus making his injuries much worse as he tried to get out before the flames caught him. Walker dragged Lewallen out of the truck and 203HE rounds began cooking off amidst the flames, sending shrapnel bouncing around inside it. Not long after, one of the LAW rockets cooked off, sending out a huge explosion inside the burning truck. Just after that explosion the Marines heard the most terrifying screams.

'I'M BURNING, I'M BURNING!!' Vega came to and began belting out in pain. To everyone's sheer shock, LCpl Vega, the turret gunner, was alive, just barely. Heat from the flames and LAW rocket explosion in the truck beside him jolted him out of unconsciousness and to his delirious terror he was trapped in an oven. Not only that, but his body was so severely injured that he struggled to even move. Walker and the others immediately started trying figure out how to get him out. Vega was screaming at them, 'Don't let me burn alive!' Walker dug out a small hole just big enough under the buried turret armor that he and the other Marines could partially see Vega. He had significant injuries and was lodged between the turret opening and the ground. There was no good way to enter the truck to reach Vega because of the growing smoke and flames so Walker called for one of the MATVs to back right up to the rear of the burning MRAP to connect to the back doors with a chain to try and rip them off. Amidst the enormous angst of racing against time to save a brother from burning to death and the chaos of having 30% of the squad in severe casualty status while still anticipating a looming enemy attack just like what happened to the Georgians, the MATV that Walker ordered to approach began to back up and pull around. What the guys in that truck didn't know is Apgar, who had been posting security behind that same MATV, had fallen unconscious again and was laid out behind one of the tires. The MATV tire started to roll up onto and over Apgar's midsection, curling his body into the tire's touchpoint on the ground and crushing his pelvis, severing his urethra, and rupturing everything else. Apgar instantly awoke with a blood-curdling scream as the tire crushed him and in the immediacy of the moment the driver heard the screams, stopped and pulled forward off Apgar. As if it all were not bad enough already. The guys on the ground quickly began to tend to Apgar, who was now really fighting for his life.

As the Apgar fiasco ensued, Vega's legs started to actually catch on fire and in what looked like a hopeless and excruciatingly painful end to his life, he began screaming at Walker to shoot him in the head and end his suffering. He was way more terrified of a slow burn than he was the quick punch of a bullet to the head. When Walker didn't take action in the speed that Vega intended, Vega lashed out at the other Marines, 'You fucking pussies! Shoot me in the head! Shoot me!! Snake me a rifle, I'll do it myself!' Unknown to Vega, Walker and Head had already been contemplating the same thing and started preparing themselves to perform the act if there was no other way. There was no outcome though that involved letting Vega slowly burn to death. Vega started losing consciousness again as the flames crawled up his legs. Walker and delirious Cline began digging frantically in one last attempt to save Vega before affirmatively making the decision to end his misery and face the repercussions of an investigation and the military court system. He and the other Marines clawed at the hard desert ground to dig a hole just barely big enough to grab Vega by his chest rig. They ripped and tugged his mangled, broken body to try to get him out while he screamed from the writhing pain. After several attempts and in such a way that unquestionably injured him much further, they yanked him fully out, saving him from burning to death, and they quickly addressed his wounds in an attempt to keep him from dying thereafter.

Many 203HE rounds and other munitions were now cooking off inside the truck in volume. Our QRF reinforcement team was still a long way away, as were the medevac helos, and the four other casualties were now feeling the pain greatly intensify as shock wore off. Doc Lewallen began administering morphine to the other guys and then hit himself with it, twice. It was now all about casualty stabilization just long enough for the medevac helo to touch down and the on-board crew to begin rendering aid. All five casualties made it onto the helo alive in what appeared nothing short of a miracle. Vega was remarkably torn up. He suffered compression fractures throughout his spine and neck, had broken ribs that were piercing into his lungs, had a broken tail bone, torn MCLs in both knees, a broken shoulder blade, severe TBI, and tattered bruising, burns, and other breaks and tears all over. He was just barely hanging on. When the medevac helo carrying the five wounded landed at Delaram, some of those receiving them thought they were all dead as they had fallen back unconscious. The trauma team quickly started working to stabilize each of them while preparing them for a quick departure to more advanced medical facilities elsewhere.

Not long after we 2nd Squad showed up to 3rd Squad's location another unit who went by call sign 'Joker' did also. They stayed long enough to hear what had happened and ensure the area was secure. Soon after they departed, they reached the edge of our horizon and then BOOM! They hit an IED three clicks away from us and within minutes of the strike dusk turned to dark, and we couldn't see their tail lights anymore. Their strike was not as detrimental though, and they were able to get out of there not too long after.

The IED strike on 3rd Squad was around 1800 and we got on scene after 1900. Despite our efforts, Command would not send an EOD team and wreckers until the following day to prevent further IED strikes in the dark, especially given Joker had just taken one also. We were on our own for the night. We sat in place around the burning MRAP watching for any signs of an ambush. The flames died down some as the night progressed, but they stayed burning still all night long. Every few minutes another grenade cooked off and shrapnel bounced around inside the truck. We sat in place all night geared up and ready to repel any attack while trading off watches on the turret guns and radios so we could all get a little sleep slumped over in our truck seats, still fully geared up. It was a very, very long night. Given that we sat staged in same place all night long and so far away from friendly forces, we suspected a likely attack the following morning. We postured ourselves for an aggressive response once the sun started to rise and watched the area closely. Hours went by with no enemy activity and around 1200 (noon) that following day the wrecker convoy finally showed up. They brought security reinforcements and an EOD team who set in some C4 control detonations and blew up all the remaining Mk19 grenades and other munitions inside the busted truck. The wreckers then rigged up what was left of the truck, and we pushed back to the FOB. We made it to Delaram around 1400, completing the twenty-hour recovery and we were all so worn out. We refueled the trucks, checked all our gear then and debriefed with Command, who gave us an update on our boys. Apgar had already undergone his first surgery at Camp Dwyer and the rest were expected to survive but Vega was still in critical condition. None of the five would return to our unit. They were only in Dwyer a short time before being flown to Bagram Air Base, where Apgar underwent his second surgery. Then they all headed to Germany and finally to San Antonio, Texas, where they remained long term. They all suffered TBIs and a laundry list of other known and newly discovered injuries. Each had long roads to recovery but many of their injuries will never fully recover.

DIVINE INTERVENTION

We left the COC and turned to. I offloaded all my gear by my rack and sat alone for a little while thinking about everything that happened. I was so physically drained and deflated. At this point in the deployment, the shock of the wartime incidents became less sharp with each occurrence. Unlike in Sangin, I was more able to disassociate from it all to some extent. Adrenaline highs and lows continued strongly, but emotional responses became less pronounced with each event.

I eventually headed to the chow hall and Garcia ran up to me on the way. He was really shaken up, which was unusual given that the typical timeframe for an event-caused emotional cycle like his was long past. We got our food and sat down, and Garcia proceeded to tell me one of the most incredible stories I have ever heard in my life.

Garcia had been moved to 3rd Squad from 2nd a few days prior to the incident. LCpl Wade, one of the 3rd Squad Marines, had been sent home to tend to a life-threatening family emergency and Garcia was selected to backfill the position. While on the patrol, Garcia was in the turret of the lead truck on the 50 cal. The patrol started out like any other but at a certain point Garcia became very uneasy. We often discussed in Sangin how the Holy Spirit sometimes burdens us to pray for things and when we feel it, we should follow through without hesitating. Garcia said that hours into their patrol, while nothing was glaringly threatening, a sudden strong urge to pray for protection came over him, so he began to pray earnestly. Sixty seconds later, the truck behind his, Clines, took the IED direct hit. Incredibly, when Garcia felt the burden and started to pray his vehicle was passing over the IED ahead of the truck that took the strike. Being in the lead truck, he and his turret gun were facing forward. Tears filled his eyes as he told me that immediately ahead of the explosion and him feeling the concussion slam into his back, the brightest white light he had ever seen came down from the sky in front of him, embraced him, and then shot behind him toward the truck that was taking the explosion, almost like an out of body experience. The blast was so huge that it knocked Garcia out of his turret seat and when he stood back up in the turret to see the immediate aftermath, he thought everyone in the truck had to be dead based on the size of the blast. The light he had just experienced made him think otherwise though. Awestruck, Garcia watched in amazement from his turret as one by one the Marines exited or were pulled out of the burning MRAP and while every one of them was badly wounded, they were all alive, even Vega.

What happened when Garcia got back to the FOB is even more astonishing. After we all returned to Delaram twenty hours after the strike, Garcia went to the MWR center (Morale, Welfare, Recreation, where computers and phones resided) to get his mind off things and there was a message in his email inbox from his mother, who was apparently fearfully concerned about Garcia. Her email asserted, 'WHAT HAPPENED AND ARE YOU OKAY!?' Garcia was obviously very confused by that; how could she have known something happened? He got her on the phone right then and she told him that while in a church service the day before, a prophetic woman approached her in tears and said, 'Something bad has happened to your son but the Lord wants to tell you that He protected him, and that he is going to be okay,' as if God wanted to put a profound confirmation on what Garcia had experienced on that patrol. I was completely blown away at hearing everything Garcia told me as I listened to this incredible account of God's miraculous hand of protection. Garcia experienced a divine burden, apparently averted disaster himself, then witnessed an angel descend into that explosion and by the mercy of God all of those in it survived. God also confirmed the entire experience through a prophetic woman on the other side of the world. I couldn't believe what I was hearing. We bowed our heads right then and earnestly thanked God for His divine intervention, for his love and concern for us, and for his mercy over Garcia and over our brothers. This was perhaps the most profound experience of the entire deployment and one of the most significant miraculous happenings I have ever been close to. I thank God to this day for it.

> *'Because he loves me,' says the Lord, 'I will rescue him. I will protect him because he acknowledges my name.'*
>
> Psalm 91:14

THE BITTER END

2nd Platoon was now down nine Marines out of our total thirty-eight. Smith and Rast were KIA, Wade was sent home on a family emergency, one of our guys was pulled from the mission for mental instability, and now Cline, Dimas, Vega, Apgar and Lewallen were severely wounded and had already left Afghanistan never to return. That was nearly 25% of 2nd Platoon thinned out. Over the month of June we continued a fast pace as the regional QRF gun trucks, chasing IED emplacements, providing a tactical taxi service running Marines to and from area outposts, and performing mounted security patrols in and around suspected enemy activity hot spots. We were undermanned and exhausted but still in the fight.

With the Drug Interdiction Mission ramping up and pressure from other Alpha Company Platoons to get into the action, decisions were made by Command that embittered me. After months of intensely strenuous operations in both Sangin and Delaram, and given our numerous casualties, Major Wood, the Alpha Company Commanding

Officer, decided to relieve 2nd Platoon as the main operating force for Alpha Company. We would soon after fall back to base security and relinquish our position as QRF to 3rd Platoon. This was enormously disappointing. Despite all our strain, we still had skin in the game. More than anything I wanted to stay actively engaged in the war. Base security was a prison sentence in comparison. When the day came, we cleared out all our gear from our trucks, 'The Tanks of Sangin' inventoried what remained of our munitions after months of repeated expenditures and replenishments, did a three-day mini-RIP (Relief in Place) with 3rd Platoon sharing insights, strategies, lessons learned and words of caution, and then officially and begrudgingly handed over the reins on our final day as 'Mesquite QRF'.

Over the remainder of the deployment Alpha Company sustained no more casualties despite numerous close calls, including very close mortar attacks on us at FOB Delaram. 3rd Platoon enacted the Drug Interdiction Mission successfully and eventually secured one of the largest opium drug busts of the entire war, which made national news back home. If we 2nd Platoon had been on it, it would have been even bigger of course, but I digress. 1st Battalion, 25th Marines showed up in early September to replace us. We RIP'd with them, passed the baton and became officially relieved of all duties in Afghanistan. Within days, we flew out of the warzone, pit-stopping at base Manas in Kyrgyzstan just as when we came in. It all felt so comforting in some ways but was so uncomfortable in many others. Everything felt both sweet and bitter at the same time; a feeling that continued for me for a very long time.

We landed in California in late September, having had the most incredible view flying over icebergs and crystal blue water in the Arctic Circle on our flight back. It was early evening when we stepped off the plane back in the States for the first time. I remember the distinct smell of the Pacific Ocean and feeling the cool fall breeze under a beautiful sunset. Four fire trucks were on the tarmac spraying their hoses into the air celebrating our return. Thirty-plus Freedom Riders were lined up on their Harley Davidsons to escort us back to Camp

Pendleton, all with American Flags affixed to the back of their bikes. We felt like heroes. Walking off that plane was one of the best feelings I have ever experienced. I didn't dare 'kiss the ground', given how ridiculously cliché it would be to do so, but I could see the appeal. We loaded onto a bus to make our way back to Pendleton. As we departed the tarmac, I turned on my cell phone for the first time in a long time and sent my parents a long-awaited confirmation that their son was finally back on American soil. I imagine the relief they felt was unlike any they'd ever experienced before. We drove to Camp Margarita on Pendleton where we lived during our months' long work-up ahead of deploying. Everything seemed just the same as before and, in many ways, it almost felt like we never left. It was all such a mind trip. It felt like the whole thing never really happened at all, a peculiar feeling that hit me over and over again and sometimes still does today.

We went through classes and briefs, addressing all the various avenues of help available to us, along with back-to-back physical and mental examinations. I remember being told, 'You may not yet feel like you've experienced the severity of mental and physical trauma that you have but rest assured you will feel it at some point and when you do, you need to know where to find help.' I thought at the time that comment was stupid and brushed it off. 'Help is for the weak, and I am not weak,' I thought … oh how wrong I was. It wasn't more than a few days before I had my first hard-hitting mental episode and quickly learned how important finding the right help during that transitional period really was. Everyone kept telling us to let our guards down. We just spent seven months doing anything but that though and it wasn't easy to relax. I felt so out of place but after a little time things began to smooth over and the idea of adjusting back to peacetime started to become more prominent in my mind. We were only at Camp Pendleton for a week before we flew home to Texas. On one of my last days in Cali before flying home I took an easy run into the mountainous training grounds that we spent our pre-deployment work-up in one last time. I journaled about the experience later that afternoon:

'We are just a couple days away from returning home. While exciting, our time back in Cali has been heavy. I went on a long run earlier today to clear my mind and ended up on some of the training grounds that we had trained so rigorously on almost a year ago as we prepared for combat. After a couple miles I became overwhelmed with emotion and broke down. In what seems like such a brief blip of time, I am right back here where it all started but rather than just beginning, it is all ending. I remember all the anticipation, anxiousness, and excitement as I looked forward to all that may occur in my fight in Afghanistan. It was all that mattered to me at that time. I was on my way to war, and I was completely committed to it and nothing else. It is as if I have come back in time and can see myself preparing for all that I was about to experience but now knowing fully all that would transpire. Now I am scarred by the brutality of all I just took part in and pained by my own hardened heart that at times was filled with the most bitterly intense hatred and desire for bloodshed. I am ashamed of that. My mind expended itself over and over on creative strategies behind acts of war that I have now committed on other human beings, and I don't feel like myself anymore. I crossed moral lines that I cannot uncross. I am back in this place that should feel normal, but I do not feel normal. I feel achieved but also expended. Will I ever make it back to this place? Will I ever step foot again in these West Coast hills where I gave away so much of myself? Maybe, but never again with all the men that were here with me, my own band of brothers. It will never be the same and I can see that. In the last year of my life this was all that mattered to me, and it is about to be gone forever. I gave away so much and what I feel like I am now reaping from my sacrifice is just more loss. I fought in my generation's war. I killed the men who opposed me and survived their relentless attempts to kill me. I did my best to hold myself to the highest standard and keep my honor clean. I should only feel victorious, but what I mostly feel is sadness.'

Painful. It was all so painful.

HOME AT LAST

On October 1, 2011, we deboarded a commercial flight from California onto the tarmac at Ellington Field in Houston, Texas, where a large crowd of extremely excited family members awaited. My parents were there to pick me up. This would be the first time in a very long time that I would be separated from my Marines, and I was nervous. Even for only a few days the guys wouldn't be there to have my six and I wouldn't be there to cover theirs. I was headed back into my home world of familiar faces and kindred relationships, but I was coming back from a violent world that none of them could understand. I knew all the comments and questions that awaited me, and I didn't know how I was going to respond to them.

We Alpha Company Marines marched in formation from the plane down a straight run lined with multitudes of American flags into the middle of the roaring crowd, where Major Wood quickly released us for liberty amidst a wave of cheers. I turned to Mathes, who had the same look of stoic angst that I had, and gave him a hug just in time for his wife to steal his attention. Moments after, my parents emerged from the crowd and my mom wrapped me up in her arms and began to cry. Dad couldn't hold his tears back either and just as soon as mom let go, he extended his hand to shake mine and wrapped his other arm around my neck, too choked up to utter a word. I kept looking around to catch other Marines' eyes as if to reassure myself that I wasn't alone. This was the most painfully ironic thing given the last time I had seen my parents in person I was struck with the same feeling but this time, their presence, and not their absence, was a part of the cause of my discomfort.

Some of SSgt Jeremy Smith's family were there to see us home. We gathered with them and personally handed Smith's journals and wedding ring to Jeremy's wife Rachel in a somber but also tremendously honoring interaction. I'm not sure how I expected it all to go but what hit me the hardest was watching Smith's dad unable to control his tears in episodes of emotion. My dad was watching his son from a distance behind us while Smith's dad was faced with another brunt reminder of the absence of his own. We were so honored that they were there though, and we assured them we would not lose touch. To this day, we still stay in contact.

The drive home from Houston with my parents was surreal. I was wound up and nervous and my mind searched restlessly for threats while we drove. I told myself to relax but as soon as I wasn't actively suppressing the urge to be fully situationally aware, I was right back into scanning my surroundings and analyzing potential threats; all amplified by my being the only Marine in the vehicle. I arrived at my parents' house to a warm welcome from loving family members very similar to how our last gathering was before I left. It felt good, but I could only take so much of it. The next few days were as off balance as anyone would expect and the nights were way worse. I didn't sleep well and frequently woke up panicking because I couldn't find my rifle, which for the past year I had either in arm's reach or literally lying beside me every single night. I also woke up in episodes of extreme angst because I didn't recognize where I was and couldn't locate my other Marines in the dark room around me.

Regular simple daily decisions were unusually difficult. I remember trying to pick which clothes to wear the first morning home and ended up in tears because I couldn't remember what shirt went best with what shorts. When I finally put shorts and a shirt on it was almost intolerably uncomfortable as they were not cammies and boots. I felt exposed and tactically underprepared to venture outside, where any number of imaginary threats did not actually await. Everything angered me, made me uncomfortable and life in general lacked any sense of real purpose. People were annoying, lazy, situationally oblivious, and boring in their meaningless comings and goings. I was finally home but all I wanted was to be back in Afghanistan.

Over the course of the following few years, I experienced the rocky transition back into civilian life. On my worst days I wished so sincerely to have just been killed in Afghanistan while I was at my warfighting prime. At least I would have gone out a hero that way. There was no life experience that came close to fulfilling me the way fighting in the GWOT did. In the Global War on Terror, there was a worldwide cry against the atrocities of evil men, and I made the conscious decision to do something about it. It was all so meaningful. Even in the mundane and tormentingly basic tasks, I was still a United States Marine; one of America's finest sons and a committed part of the fiercest fighting force in the world. Honor, Courage, and Commitment were my highest values, and my life motto was *Semper Fidelis,* Always Faithful. I was brashly determined to be the best and was devoted to my Corps. I achieved the highest aspiration of a young Marine by engaging in combat. When I returned home, I was received as a war hero. Moving on from such a climactic life experience was so difficult and starting over with anything else in the civilian world seemed like a waste of time. It took me years to figure out how to enjoy a new life direction and stick with it long enough to become successful and fulfilling.

With each new year passing now my time in the Marine Corps becomes more distant in memory. 'Once a Marine, always a Marine,' is one of the most prominent branding phrases marketed by the Corps and while cliché for sure, it means something to me. The Marine mentality I forged through the firestorm of my time in the brotherhood has changed some over the years but not in every way. I've matured and continue to, but I'll carry the marks of a Marine on my inner man until the day I die.

> *'Sometimes you find yourself in the middle of nowhere. Sometimes in the middle of nowhere you find yourself.'*
>
>   Jeremy Smith

Chapter 10

WAR AND HUMANITY

'The price of freedom may be high, but never so costly as the loss of freedom.'

Ronald Reagan

It has been more than a decade since my involvement in the war and I still look back on it all with a heavy heart and swirl of emotion. The cost of life was high on both sides of those blood-stained poppy fields and the tragedy of it is at times not easy to think about. The burden weighs on me still, as I am sure it does many others. I think I would be even more burdened living with an acknowledgement of willful inaction had I chosen to not be a part of it though. I am proud of the decision I made in joining America's military. Becoming a Marine and fighting in my generation's war was one of the greatest opportunities I had to make a positive difference in this world. For me it was all about defending the free way of life that I cherish, liberating others into the same and upholding justice in the world against the terrorists that murdered the innocent and warred against us.

As I get older and recognize the youthful ignorance of my late teens and early twenties, I've thought at times about the young enemy fighters who stood on the opposite end of my battlefields. Many of them grew up being indoctrinated from their early childhood on the call to jihad and the promise of a virgin-filled paradise awaiting them if they killed infidels to advance their leadership's twisted vision of coercive dominance in the world. Many of them died while being too young to really question the broader merits of their mission and learn to think for themselves given their confined upbringing and detachment from the outside modern world. I have to imagine that there would have been many who would later turn from the sadistic warpath they were on upon realizing how heinously abusive to others and self-serving it all was. We all have things we look back on with sincere regret in life and people do change as they get older. That said, allowing the continued spread of their tyranny was certainly not an acceptable option and there must be accountability in the world. The greater tragedy is the US service members who were killed or maimed in the war they did not start. At the very least, their honorable sacrifices were on behalf of ideals that establish liberty for the masses rather than dominance and oppressive control of the same.

Of the struggles I went through transitioning back into civilian life, one of the hardest was losing my brotherhood of Marines. A unit of Marines becomes more like family than many actual families given the way life happens in the Corps. We spend twenty-four hours a day together, often seven days a week. We wake up together, eat breakfast together, work out together, go to work together, train together, eat dinner together, go to sleep together and even spend time off together, day in and day out. There is nowhere to hide from one another and very seldom is there ever time alone. This means everyone knows everyone in an extremely in-depth way. The constant proximity and lack of closeness to people outside of the unit creates a reliance on one another that exceeds the bonds of most relationships. We all become so in tune with each other, whether we want to or not. Amplifying that effect so much further is the shared reliance of one another in war. No battlefield gets won without the team's collective effort and no single warfighter survives battle without the guys around him. Each of us were each other's lines of defense. We looked out for one another.

This all results in extremely tight relational bonds of brotherhood and transitioning away from it was very difficult.

Participating in the war was both rewarding and costly. I am not the same person I was before going to war. In some ways I am stronger than before; more resolute in my actions, more determined in my decisions and more compassionate in my understanding of humanity and the plights that people find themselves in. In other ways my inner man has been scarred, my tendencies are now more rigid, my bent is more critical and my outlook on life more despondent at times than I care to admit. I achieved my greatest childhood aspiration of becoming a United States Marine, which was in my youthful eyes the single highest representation of excellence. In performing my wartime duties as a Marine, though, I crossed moral boundaries, which uprooted foundations of my identity and imprinted convoluted darkness in place.

As a Christian, I struggled with fundamental contradictions. I was constantly trying to balance godliness with my duties as a Marine, and they often conflicted. I could justify fighting and killing in defense of a greater good, and especially given OEF was in response to real attacks that destroyed innocent lives and credible threats of more, but the heart posture behind the fighting was a struggle. G.K. Chesterton is credited with the quote, 'The true soldier fights not because he hates what is in front of him, but because he loves what is behind him.' There is truth in that. I joined the Marine Corps out of sincere love and appreciation for my country. I had a good heart and was resolved to be a peacemaker the way God wanted me to be. The rigors of war are overpowering though. Effectively acting out the commission of violence can require a tremendous amount of mental and emotional positioning. To not crumble from guilt in killing or hesitate and be killed, you almost must hate your enemy or at least devalue their humanity, which is not much better. I think this is because God didn't design any of us to carry the burdens of war as war was never a part of his original intent for humanity. War resulted from mankind's fall from grace and has roots as deep as Cain's infamous murder of Abel in the book of Genesis.

War is one of the greatest tragedies of humanity and after having committed myself to it for years and partaken in its actions, I really disdain it to the extent that it results in severe human suffering and the excessive destruction of lives. I will, however, never succumb to the hopeful temptation of believing that this world will ever be without it. War is inevitable because evil in the human heart is ultimately incurable in this life. The history of humanity is filled with man's seizure of self-benefit through the control of others. When left unchecked, tyrannical oppression and abuse of the worst kinds will always manifest. It takes a strong resistance and proactivity from moral people to combat this kind of evil and that will always be.

Ahead of committing myself to the Marine Corps I was fully aware of the privilege I had in being born an American. America is a dream world compared to the rest of the planet. Of all people who have lived and died on this earth there has never been a group more collectively privileged than citizens of the United States of America and that is largely because this nation has held freedom and justice among its highest values. America has been a light in this dark world, not without error and even some egregious, but no country has ever been faultless. In the history of the world there has not been a nation more positively impactful toward the freedom and prosperity of humanity as the United States, which is why millions of people all around the world go to extreme lengths just to get here. In America, the land of the free, resides the greatest potential for any individual in any echelon of society to build, advance and prosper, and not by way of tyrannizing others. Our way of life has been regularly paid for from one generation to the next with the blood of American patriots, and if not for them the quality of our existence would be questionable today.

The Global War on Terror was a new kind of war for America. Afghanistan in particular was certainly not the all-out conventional war like many of the past, but it was very much war. It was battlefield force on force, hunter and hunted, killing, and being killed. Both victories and defeats involved America's men and women, and many were very young like I was. It is important to always remember that none of us were forced to go. Everyone volunteered. It was a chance to be a part of a valiant effort to defend ourselves against the terrorists who sought to destroy us and our way of life. It was also an opportunity to liberate oppressed people who suffered heinous abuses under the control of those terrorists and to give the oppressed a chance to enjoy their lives free of others' tyranny like we did. For these great causes, many of America's most honorable men and women took upon their own shoulders the burdens of war, enduring great pains and suffering crippling tragedies to shield others from having to experience the same and worse. We accepted the risks, persevered through the hardships, and expended ourselves in many ways that are beyond recovery. We did it all because it was worth doing.

Many question what it is about our country that is so great; what espouses America with honor and why this nation and our way of life is worth all the sacrifice. They should also ask why freedom and equal justice are so precious and held so sacred to those of us willing to give all in their defense. There are different ways to respond to each of these questions, but I think the most impactful answer resides in the simplest terms. The ultimate reason is that the highest and best existence for any human being is one that is fundamentally free of other people's unwanted control, and that within a society that upholds justice evenly for everyone. In no other nation has this been more widely established for longer periods of time than in the United States of America. America was built around the simple idea that all people are born with God-given rights that entitle them to live their lives freely on their own terms, while themselves not encroaching on the freedoms of others. This bedrock value has reaped us blessing upon blessing ever since it was embedded in our founding. There is a line in the Declaration of Independence that says, 'We hold these truths to be self-evident, that all men are created equal, that they are endowed by their Creator with certain unalienable rights, that among these are life, liberty and the pursuit of happiness.'[14] The entire document, which effectively became a declaration of war at the time it was written, stated in specific terms that the American people refused to subject themselves any longer to the unaccountable tyranny of others. They declared themselves free and then fought their oppressors to the death in defense of that declaration. Great sacrifice and extreme difficulty were embraced for the sake of establishing our way of life. Those of us alive today are the benefactors of what those men and women courageously started. Each generation from then to now has had and will have the opportunity to either continue or squelch the freedoms they've been given. I hope from the bottom of my heart enough people today recognize this and choose the former.

I thank God for allowing me to be a part of my generation's war and to contribute with great effort toward the establishment and continuation of freedom and justice in this challenging world. I thank Him more for sending Jesus to pay the just price for my sin, allowing me to experience eternal freedom, the highest and best existence for every human soul forever.

I am a Untied States Marine and American warfighter. Perhaps more important than both of those, I am so grateful to just be an American. May God bless all who've opened this book. May He lift his presence upon you, be gracious to you and give you peace. Thank you for your time and attention.

---

14. Declaration of Independence.

FOR THE FALLEN

For the fallen but not forgotten, the lives that are no more
For those who fought and died on battlefields far from home
For their selfless dedication to the establishment of peace
For their courage and resolve to fight and die free
For their pain and suffering across days of endless unrest
For their righteous indignation against
oppression and injustice
For the victories they achieved, most remain untold
For their crippling tragedies that we will never know
For those they left behind now afflicted by their loss
Whose pain will never fully heal, they still
pay the highest cost

In a world that asks so much of so few relative to the whole
Apathy and impartiality are the greatest insults of all
To the many that live on indifferent, uninterested or unaware
A price was paid for your indifference, and that by volunteers
Honorable men and women took up a mantle offered to all
To defend what is right and just in this world despite
the potential cost

May their names always be remembered,
and their stories frequently told
That others will emulate their example
to be honorable, courageous and bold
To the fallen but not forgotten, fair winds and following seas
May you enter eternal freedom, good luck and godspeed

'Freedom has a taste to those who have fought and almost died that the protected will never know'

May all those who've sacrificed their lives for others experience eternal freedom from all this world's sorrows.

Landon Longgrear

RIFLEMAN'S CREED

THIS IS MY RIFLE.

There are many like it, but this one is mine. My rifle is my best friend. It is my life. I must master it as I must master my life.

My rifle, without me, is useless. Without my rifle, I am useless. I must fire my rifle true. I must shoot straighter than my enemy who is trying to kill me. I must shoot him before he shoots me. I will.

My rifle and myself know that what counts in this war is not the rounds we fire, the noise of our bursts, nor the smoke we make. We know that it is the hits that count. We will hit.

My rifle is human, even as I, because it is my life. Thus, I will learn it as a brother. I will learn its weaknesses, its strength, its parts, its accessories, its sights, and its barrel. I will keep my rifle clean and ready, even as I am clean and ready. We will become part of each other. We will.

Before God, I swear this creed. My rifle and myself are the defenders of my country. We are the masters of our enemy. We are the saviors of my life.

So be it, until victory is America's and there is no enemy, but peace.

Major General William H. Rupertus